Y0-BVE-742

HERE'S WHAT THEY'VE SAID ABOUT JIM SHAW:

"It gave us a breakthrough perspective on how the organization functions. It enabled us to focus on the key processes as the patient sees them...It is not a fad—we're still using it more than four years later."

—Dr. David Druker,
Chief Operating Officer, Palo Alto Foundation

"The Process Profile® [diagram]...got the organization to think about how processes flow across the organization. This was a new idea...It focuses you on the data that are important to customers."

—Chris Menicou
Director, Digital Quality—LTX Trillium

"When you measure it, it becomes important. And once you've used Jim's Process Profile® [diagram] to define the process, you've created the ability to measure the process."

—Roger Hite
Chief Operating Officer, Dominican Santa Cruz Hospital

"This way of looking at defects and quality—from the customer's perspective—makes sense to us, and we're applying these principles every day."

—Lisa Kalmbach
President, Kaufman and Broad—South Bay, Inc.

CUSTOMER-INSPIRED
QUALITY

Looking Backward
Through the Telescope

James G. Shaw

Jossey-Bass Publishers • San Francisco

Copyright © 1996 by James G. Shaw

All rights reserved. No part of this book may be reproduced, stored in a retrieval system, or transmitted, in any form or by any means, electronic, mechanical, photocopying, recording, or otherwise, without the prior written permission of the publisher.

"Process Profile®" is a registered trademark of Shaw Resources. In reprinting, the registration mark must be used, accompanied by the note "Reg. U.S. Pat. & Tm. Off.," the first time the term is used. In subsequent uses, the term must be distinguished by a typeface different from the text. Note that trademarks are to be used as adjectives, not as nouns or verbs.

Substantial discounts on bulk quantities of Jossey-Bass books are available to corporations, professional associations, and other organizations. For details and discount information, contact the special sales department at Jossey-Bass Inc., Publishers (415) 433-1740; Fax (800) 605-2665.

For sales outside the United States, please contact your local Simon & Schuster International office.

Jossey-Bass Web address: http://www.josseybass.com

Manufactured in the United States of America.

Library of Congress Cataloging-in-Publication Data

Shaw, James G.
    Customer inspired quality / James G. Shaw
        p.   cm—(Warren Bennis executive briefing series)
    Includes index.
    ISBN: 0-7879-0346-9 (hardcover)
    1. Leadership   I. Title   II. Series

HB Printing   10 9 8 7 6 5 4 3 2

Dedication

For my wife Barbara

Contents

Editor's Preface

The business literature today is full of exhortations to organizations to reexamine and reinvent themselves. Process improvement and process reengineering are hot topics. Organizations are trying to learn how to be "learning" organizations, how to implement cross-functional teams, how to flatten their hierarchies, and so on. Part of this is a search for strategies and practices that will enable organizations to survive in an increasingly complex, competitive, and global marketplace. Part of it is the realization that the "quality" issues raised a few decades ago really apply to all aspects of the organization, not just to the output of the assembly line.

There is one element in all of this that needs to be focused, and that is the purpose of all this effort. Obviously, the survival of the organization is the ultimate goal, with the prosperity of the organization a close second. But if the "bottom line" is the only recognized motivator, the organization is quite likely to miss the target.

All organizations exist to serve clients or customers of some type. It is those clients or customers who ultimately decide the fate of the organization, by their responses to its products and/or services. So if the organization fails to include the customers' point of view in its planning and organizing efforts, it is likely to miss the mark and suffer the consequences.

Jim Shaw has built his career around teaching organizations how to define and improve their inputs, their processes, and their outputs from the point of view of the customer. More importantly, he teaches organizations how to define "quality" from the customers' viewpoint. In *Customer-Inspired Quality*, he tells us exactly what we need to do to ensure that our efforts are focused on and directed toward meeting the expectations of our internal and external customers.

Shaw provides a step-by-step process for creating a profile of any organizational process and for using process-improvement teams to improve it so that it results in quality output—as defined by the customer of the process. His methodology can be applied to service and administrative processes as well as to manufacturing processes.

Shaw's methodology doesn't require organizations to stop working in order to reform themselves; it is an ongoing improvement process that becomes part of the work. I'm pleased to see it become part of the knowledge disseminated through the *Bennis Executive Briefing Series.*

Warren Bennis
University of Southern California

Author's Preface

In the twenty years that I spent bringing customer-driven process improvement to high-technology and manufacturing organizations, I gradually realized that the principles and processes I taught would apply equally well to service and administrative processes. So for the past eight years, I've been trying to do just that. I have had the satisfaction of guiding a variety of organizations in their efforts to achieve quality and create customer-driven perspectives.

Customer-Inspired Quality was sparked by questions from numerous process owners during the course of my work with senior managers and improvement teams from a variety of industries, including banking, high-technology, manufacturing, construction, education/research, and general service.

There are two overall messages in this book. The first is that virtually no organization can afford to ignore its customers' needs and desires. But, too often, organizations try to define quality for their customers, rather than asking their customers what they perceive as quality in a specific product or service. The second is that process improvement is the only known way to make real, long-lasting changes in an organization that will increase its chances of survival and prosperity. In this book, I try to show how to introduce process improvement in an organization in a way that quantitatively measures results and gives management real numbers that can be used for cost/benefit assessments.

I particularly want to acknowledge my health care clients, who were the first in their industry to prove that the methodology described in this book could be successful in health care. At the time they adopted it, the health care industry was just awakening to the concept that patients are customers and, as customers, are the final judges of the quality of care they receive.

Special thanks to all the employees of the San Jose Medical Group, which was the first health care organization to internalize the methodology. I also want to acknowledge Mr. Robert Boyle and Dr. David Drucker of the Palo Alto Medical Foundation, Sr. Julie Hyer and Mr. Roger Hite of Dominican Santa Cruz Hospital, Ms. Nancy Farber of Washington Hospital, and Mr. Wayne New of Driscoll Children's Hospital.

In addition, I want to thank my colleagues Dena McFarland and Hal Moyers, who contributed many thoughtful hours, clarifying the details of the methodology and providing constructive feedback that was immensely helpful.

Finally, I want to thank Patricia Carr, who spent many hours editing the manuscript for me before it was submitted to a publisher. Her questions led to many of the practical examples used to illustrate the methodology. She also found many of the quotations used in the book. She more than met the challenge given to her.

James G. Shaw
Cupertino, California

Foreword

Today's economy has forced many businesses to focus on the spread sheet. To many, the most expedient solution seems to be downsizing and cutting costs to make the business more profitable. All this attention paid to the bottom line has blinded managers to what should be their main focus: the customer. It is the customer who has the power to change the profit/loss figures in an annual report. Only by listening to the customer can one hope to make a solid, lasting, and profitable change in business.

By focusing on the customer, one is really concentrating on serving and satisfying the customer's needs. Customer satisfaction creates customer retention which, in turn, means profitability. It sounds like an easy answer, but it involves a commitment—a commitment to make service the number-one priority. It also means changing the traditional management style: moving decision making from the management level to the front-line-employee level.

As Jim Shaw cogently points out in this book, customer satisfaction is inextricably linked to profitability: you must keep your customers, and to keep them you must make them happy. Total quality management (TQM) provides a system that allows you to do both.

In the hospitality industry, the product is service; it is the cornerstone of The Ritz-Carlton Hotel Company. Therefore, every position in a hotel is a service position, and every employee a service professional. One must be careful to differentiate between service and servant: to serve is an honor. Ritz-Carlton employees are not servants. Instead, as our motto states, our employees are "Ladies and gentlemen serving ladies and gentlemen." In fact, our "Credo" and our "Twenty Basics" support the dignity of our profession—a profession that, it is estimated, will employ one in every nine workers worldwide this year.

In today's competitive climate, where technology, global travel, and the cross-cultural sharing of goods and ideas can homogenize many products, it is providing quality from the customer's point of view that distinguishes one company, hotel, or manufacturer from another. I believe that customer service—meeting and exceeding the customer's needs—is the key to success or failure for an organization.

Of course, technological advances are important, and their benefits cannot be ignored. At The Ritz-Carlton, we use an advanced computer system to store our guest recognition program. This program allows us to track the preferences of all our guests so that when a guest requests a down pillow at The Ritz-Carlton, Sydney, she automatically has one in her room when she checks into The Ritz-Carlton, Cancun, six months later.

However, it always comes back to the human element. To determine these preferences, we are dependent on the attentiveness of the front-line employee to listen to a request or to anticipate the needs of a guest. It is that employee's commitment to guaranteeing a flawless experience that makes the guest recognition program successful. This process, noting and anticipating the wishes of our customers, is very important. When employees embrace customer satisfaction, they strive to meet the customer's needs in advance. This focus on anticipating the customer's desires is "customer-inspired quality" in action. It sets an organization apart from the others in its field.

In addition to serving our guests, our employees must also be allowed to satisfy them, to answer their requests, comply with their wishes, and correct any type of situation. This is called empowerment. The front-line employees are the ones who know what the customers want because they interact with the customers on a daily basis. That is why our employees are empowered to make decisions without waiting for their managers' permission. The results are immediate.

Now that we have established that quality service is the most important component of the future of business, and that empowered employees are the most important aspect of providing quality service, we must ensure that a system is in place to support and to guarantee that service. Our organizational systems must be able to handle any request and still maintain consistent quality of service, no matter what the challenge or situation.

This brings me back to the subject of this book. The need to provide quality service requires constantly redesigning products and services so that the customers get what they want. If the customers' needs change, you must have a system in place that tells you quickly how to design new products and services. This system is total quality management. This book tells you how to use TQM to improve your systems and processes so that you are able to deliver quality service that meets and exceeds the customer's expectations.

The most important lesson to be learned from TQM is "never stop learning." The quality movement is beneficial to all industries because the systems and practices can cross over by means of a process called "benchmarking." This proves that service is a universal concept, no matter what the business.

Pursuing and then winning the Malcolm Baldrige National Quality Award in 1992 taught us that we cannot remain at one level of customer satisfaction. We must strive continually to improve ourselves, our service, and our systems. TQM is not a solution; it is a never-ending process, a system of continuous improvement. The secret simply is hard work and a continual striving to be the best—to be more efficient, more service driven, and more profitable. The refusal to be complacent creates flexibility and stimulates the drive to put systems in place that continually adapt to the changing needs of today's customers, today's economy, and today's society.

Horst S. Schulze
President and Chief Operating Officer,
The Ritz-Carlton Hotel Company, L.L.C.

LOOKING BACKWARD THROUGH THE TELESCOPE

Introduction

Although many organizations spend a great deal of time peering into the marketplace with a telescope, trying to focus on the customers they want to have, few organizations turn the telescope around and attempt to look backward at themselves from the customers' point of view. However, that is the only perspective that allows you to see what it is about your product or service that is important to your customers.

The message in business literature is that organizations need to be "customer driven," but what does that mean and how do you achieve it? *Customer-Inspired Quality* answers these questions. It is a practical guide, packed with procedures for identifying customer expectations, developing performance measurements based on these expectations, and evaluating an organization's processes in order to meet and exceed these expectations.

Exceeding customer expectations results in "quality," from the customer's point of view. And that is the point of view that counts when it comes to bottom-line results.

PROBLEM SOLVING IS NOT THE ANSWER

Quality issues rarely are the result of mistakes or poor performance by people. They usually are difficulties embedded in the processes and systems of the organization. Until now, attempts to improve quality have focused on solving isolated problems, using various quality-improvement tools such as statistical process control and flow charts. The fact is that problem solving may have little or no impact on the elements that define quality for the customer, and problem solving certainly has no ability to inspire changes that prevent problems from recurring or happening in the first place.

The first step of process improvement is, of course, to list what the processes are. The procedures set forth in this book assume that management already has identified the organization's key processes. Chapter 1 begins at the point where management is ready to start work on improving an individual process.

It is often a difficult thing to do, to look at yourself objectively from someone else's perspective. *Customer-Inspired Quality* makes it possible for you to use a proven, proprietary methodology that has helped many different organizations achieve results with process improvement. For process improvement to be continuous, for quality to reach excellence and stay there, people within the organization have to carry on after the initial kick-off phase. This book not only helps executives launch a process-improvement initiative, it provides information and tips on how to continue to obtain real results in a real world.

Much of the literature on process improvement is devoted to manufacturing processes, which is not surprising, as the quality movement began on the factory floor. But this narrow slant ignores the needs of the service sector—which now makes up two-thirds of the U.S. economy—and the service and administrative functions of manufacturing environments. The procedures in this book address the needs of service industries as well as manufacturing organizations.

OBJECTS MAY BE CLOSER THAN THEY APPEAR

Most people use a telescope to examine objects that are at a distance, so most people would not think about using a telescope to look at themselves. But in trying to define quality from the customers' point of view, that is exactly what must be done. To become customer driven, you must step outside your organization, take the stance of the customer, and look back at how the organization appears to function to the outside world.

The search for quality and excellence is embedded in the intricate processes of the organization, how work gets done and how these activities affect and are interpreted by customers. The bases of quality may be closer than they appear. So get ready to refocus your telescope on a new target: your organization and how it can achieve customer-inspired quality.

Many organizations solve problem after problem without improving the processes in which the problems emerge. Such organizations are always hanging on the edge of a cliff. They invest large sums of money without significant return. After solving numerous problems, they ultimately discover that they are in approximately the same place as when they started.

This chapter discusses some basic things you will need to know in order to get off the cliff edge and points you in the direction of improving processes in ways that count.

GETTING OFF THE CLIFF EDGE

Each problem solved introduces a new unsolved problem.

Anonymous (U.S. Department of Labor)

1

A DEFINITION OF PROCESS IMPROVEMENT

Process improvement is a way of applying logic to work. It is a rational, systematic approach to work—to the way in which work is done.

A process is a series of logically related activities performed to achieve a specific outcome. There is a process to purchase office supplies, a process to admit patients to a hospital, and so on.

Process improvement requires an iterative methodology for making changes to the process so as to raise the customer's judgment of the outcome. To improve a process, you need to do the following:

- ◆ "Walk through" the process from beginning to end and back again, eliminating obvious variations and defects in order to bring the process under control and make it more predictable;

♦ Cycle back to the beginning to start streamlining or simplifying the process to make it more efficient, and after that;

♦ Cycle back to make the process error free, and then continue in a recurrent loop of continuous improvement.

It is necessary to stress that the walk-through must be done in the shoes of the customer. (This is discussed in more detail in Chapter 2.)

PREVENTION VS. PROBLEM SOLVING

Many organizations confuse process improvement and problem solving. They think that if they find a problem in the process and fix it, they're improving the process. This is how a good many so-called process-improvement efforts have ended up on the edge of a cliff.

Finding and fixing problems is too
piecemeal an approach for enduring
process improvement.

The problem with the problem-solving approach is its piecemeal nature, the failure to consider how solutions relate to one another and to the whole. An improvement team is often charged with solving a particular, visible problem without being given a chance to understand the process in which that problem is embedded. Consequently, the team can't see all the pieces and is apt to fix the problem without making changes that would eliminate the problem once and for all.

Such individual solutions don't add up to significant gains because they are isolated solutions, often unconnected to the overall goals of the organization. Such solutions may even be counterproductive.

Production is not the application of tools to materials, but logic to work.

—Peter S. Drucker

In contrast, improving processes prevents problems. By understanding your process in terms of its outcome and the activities that produce the outcome, you can see both the whole of the process and its parts. You can see how changes to one activity will affect the others. You can diagnose the process and bring it under control. You can make changes to the process that will eliminate existing problems and prevent them from recurring.

CONTINUOUS IMPROVEMENT VS. ACCEPTABLE DEFECT LEVELS

The idea of continuous improvement may be new to organizations that are accustomed to thinking in terms of acceptable defect levels. Acceptable defect levels vary a good deal. For example, a hospital might allow sixty to seventy errors per hundred statements, but only one error per hundred blood tests.

Organizations that allow acceptable defect levels may not be aware of the proliferating costs of a defect. A defect may cost the organization one dollar in the design phase, ten dollars by the time it reaches manufacturing, one hundred dollars when it is shipped, and one thousand dollars by the time it reaches the customer. The costs of defects can spiral out of control even when acceptable defect levels are low.

An assumption behind "continuous improvement" is that defects always can be reduced. An organization might set a goal of reducing statement errors to 50 percent over the first month, 40 percent over the following month, and so on. Even very low defect levels can be reduced. In the second example above, the one error per 100 blood tests could be reduced the first month to .75, the second month to .50, then to .25, and so on.

Some organizations also set performance standards and quotas as a way to

If you wish to make an improved product, you must already be engaged in making an inferior one.

—Jacob A. Varela

improve productivity. Management may issue a fiat to increase production from 100 documents per hour to 105 per hour. But fiats have little to do with productivity. Only changes in the process will improve productivity.

Defect reduction is only a part of process improvement. Customer perceptions and preferences are vital (and are discussed more comprehensively in Chapter 2).

WHY IMPROVE PROCESSES?

The reason that organizations want to improve is because they know that something isn't working as well as it could.

An organization consists of its processes. Making things work better means improving the work processes.

WORK PROCESSES VS. THE ORGANIZATIONAL CHART

Many people think of an organization in terms of its hierarchical organization chart. But an organizational chart describes the chain of command, not the work

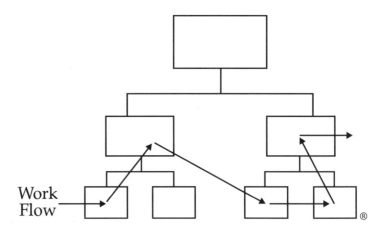

Work Flow and the Organizational Chart

Reg. U.S. Pat. & Tm. Off. A registered trademark of Shaw Resources.

processes. The organizational chart is constructed vertically; work flows through the organization in a more horizontal fashion. Because the organizational chart depicts power and control, not how work gets done, it is of little use in improving processes. It can even get in the way, creating barriers and territorial disputes. Executives sometimes tend to adjust the organizational chart rather than improve their work processes.

Managing horizontally means focusing on a process and its outputs to the customer instead of on a department and its reporting structure. Managing horizontally means recognizing the interdependencies of processes and avoiding the parochial, fragmented approach depicted in the organizational chart. Managing horizontally means taking the broad perspective and keeping the customer clearly in view.

What needs to be improved is the way in which work is done, not the people who do the work.

IMPROVE PROCESSES, NOT PEOPLE

Adjusting the organizational chart is part of a tendency to assume that people are the problem when something is wrong. Certain people are perceived to be incompetent, or have a bad attitude, or lack motivation.

More often than not, however, processes are the problem, not people. Nearly all people come to work wanting to do a good job. What needs to be improved is the way in which the work is done, not the people who do the work. Doing this involves making changes to the processes so that people can do a good job.

At least 85 percent of an organization's problems can be solved by improving its processes. Appropriate job-skills training will solve another 10 percent. Only about 5 percent of an organization's problems are actually "people problems."

The organizational chart also tends to encourage the mistaken idea that only managers are capable of identifying and making improvements. This assumption overlooks the valuable resource residing in the work force. Workers know their own work processes best and will suggest excellent ways to improve them when given the chance.

LEADERSHIP

Although workers can contribute importantly to process improvement, the responsibility for the organization's processes belongs to management. Therefore, management needs to be accountable for improving processes.

Organizations that initiate process-improvement efforts sometimes are tempted to turn over the responsibility to outside experts. "We'll hire a consultant to improve things."

THE FAR SIDE   By GARY LARSON

The Far Side cartoon by Gary Larson is reprinted by permission of Chronicle Features, San Francisco, CA. All rights reserved.

"Say ... Look what THEY'RE DOING."

Executives within the organization who are accountable for results should lead the process-improvement effort.

Outside experts cannot lead an improvement effort because they do not have a personal stake in the success of the effort. The responsibility for process improvement cannot be delegated. Improving a process requires the leadership of a person in the organization who is accountable for results, preferably an executive whose own success is linked to the success of the effort. This is the level of commitment needed in order to achieve significant and long-lasting results.

Moreover, sooner or later an outside expert goes home. Then what? A process is never optimized. It can and must be continually improved. Only the people on the payroll, from the top down, can establish a permanent culture of continuous improvement.

Our approach is to teach all people in the organization how to improve processes so that they can sustain a continuous-improvement effort on their own.

BENEFITS

People often assume that improving processes is expensive. Actually, improving processes leads to lower costs. Improving a process reduces the resources needed to generate an outcome while increasing the outcome's predictability. Studies consistently show that eliminating rework and unnecessary work, shortening cycle times, reducing defects—all the streamlining activities of process improvement—result in lower costs and higher productivity. It is not unusual for a process to show a 25 percent reduction in costs within the first year of an improvement initiative. An ongoing continuous-improvement effort can yield additional annual savings of 4 to 6 percent.

The biggest benefit of improving processes is satisfied customers.

Improving processes also focuses management and the work force on clearly defined, objective goals held in common. Process improvement provides a systemic approach to making changes and fosters cooperative work, which enhances job satisfaction and commitment.

The biggest benefit of improving processes, however, is satisfied customers. The improvement of an organization's work processes improves what customers receive, and it is by what they receive that customers judge an organization.

CULTURAL CHANGE

Improving processes may require and inspire a cultural change in an organization. Conventional wisdom may have to give way to new concepts.

Conventional Wisdom	New Concept
Quality is meeting conformance standards. *or* Quality is an intangible good.	Quality is meeting and exceeding customer expectations. *or* Quality is defined by the customer.
Finding and fixing problems results in improvements, which may or may not be sustainable.	Making changes to the system to prevent problems results in sustainable improvements.
Effectiveness and efficiency are achieved by meeting acceptable defect levels.	Effectiveness and efficiency are achieved by continually improving.
Crisis management is the dominant management mode.	Preventative management is the dominant management mode.
Performance standards and quotas improve productivity.	Changes in the process improve productivity.
Defects are caused by workers.	Defects are caused by flaws in the process, and management is responsible for the process.
Decisions are made by "superiors."	Decisions are made through collaboration between staff and management.
Top management evaluates the organization on financial performance alone.	Top management focuses on process performance and customer satisfaction as well as on financial performance.
Process improvement is expensive.	Process improvement leads to lower costs.

Conventional Wisdom	New Concept
Only managers are capable of identifying and making improvements.	Workers know the process best and will suggest excellent ways to improve it when given a chance.
Managers command functional "fiefdoms" and are concerned with directing and controlling.	Team leaders guide cross-functional improvement teams and are concerned with planning and prevention.
Employees receive instructions and information from above, as deemed appropriate by management.	Management shares information with employees on a routine basis and on request.
Leadership for an improvement effort can be delegated to outside experts.	Leadership for an improvement effort is provided by executives within the organization, who are accountable for results.
Reviews are necessary only when things go wrong.	Regularly scheduled performance-improvement reviews are a key to improved processes.

HOW PROCESSES ARE IMPROVED

Ultimately, improving a process is a matter of taking things out rather than putting things in. Usually, simpler is better.

The first step in improving a process is to reduce the variations in the outputs. An output is a product, document, service, or information generated by the process and received by a customer. An output of a "purchase office supplies" process would be an order. An output of an "admit patients" process would be the arrival of the patient in the correct ward.

To illustrate how reducing variation improves a process, we will use the example of a hamburger, the

If your next pot of chili tastes better, it is probably because of something you left out, rather than added.

—Hal John Wimberly

Courtesy of McDonald's Corporation

output of a "cook hamburgers" process. When one cooked hamburger weighs .25 pounds and another weighs .35 pounds, they vary by .10 pounds. Similarly, if one hamburger takes five minutes to cook, while another takes eight, the cooking times vary by three minutes. If you are in the business of cooking hamburgers for customers, you would be wise to reduce these variations in order to produce a consistent product at a consistent cost. This makes it easier to teach your employees how long to cook the hamburgers, and you are more likely to produce a consistent product for your customers. When all customers receive the same quality of hamburger in the same amount of time, you are more likely to meet their minimal expectations. At the same time, your costs remain stable and predictable.

*An improved process
is more consistent.*

Process improvement begins by identifying and understanding the variations in process outputs and then making changes that reduce those variations.

SERVICE PROCESSES ARE DIFFERENT FROM MANUFACTURING PROCESSES

The universe is intractably squiggly.

—Charles Suhor

The universe of service processes is indeed "intractably squiggly," as many a front-line employee will testify. Manufacturing processes occupy a more predictable, more concrete universe.

DIFFERENT OUTPUTS

One difference between manufacturing processes and service processes is in outputs. The outputs of manufacturing processes are tangible goods, e.g., automobiles, shirts, lamps. The outputs of service processes are less tangible or intangible, e.g., the investment of money or the compilation of a vacation itinerary. Some service-process outputs are intended to create a feeling in the customer. "It's the way we make you feel that makes us the world's favorite airline," says one advertisement.

The quality of the outputs of service processes has a powerful effect on customers. If the delivery person for a new washing machine is surly and installs the machine improperly, the customer perceives poor quality, even if the washing machine itself has zero defects.

DIFFERENT INPUTS AND SUPPLIERS

The inputs of service and manufacturing processes differ, too. An input is a product, service, or information needed to perform the activities of the process and create the outputs.

Typically, a service process deals with many different kinds of inputs, some of them unexpected. For example, a travel agency requires inputs from its customers—information about where they want to go, when they want to leave and return, how they want to pay, and so on. There are many opportunities for variations in such inputs because they are supplied by the customer, and customers' needs vary.

All processes have suppliers. A supplier is the source of an input. The suppliers to manufacturing processes generally fall into two categories: the first is vendors who provide materials; the second is groups within the organization that supply parts, documents, or other inputs needed to create the product.

Service processes have these types of suppliers, too. In addition, however,

The suppliers to service processes almost always include customers.

Service processes usually need something from the customer to be "processed." A bank customer supplies deposits, a patient supplies a medical need, and a life insurance customer supplies personal data. This is why service processes often have more variations in inputs than do manufacturing processes.

Moreover, these variations are to be accommodated, not corrected, as would be the case in a manufacturing process. In manufacturing, a component that is installed upside down is a variation that needs to be corrected. The supplier could add a beveled edge to the component so that it can be installed in only one way. However, the variations in customer inputs, which always come from outside the process, usually require response, not correction. One customer of a travel agency may be primarily cost conscious, while another's priority may be to travel as comfortably as possible.

A PREDICTABLE YET FLEXIBLE PROCESS

The challenge in improving service processes is to have a process predictable enough to be under control yet flexible enough to respond as necessary to numerous individual requirements. The "squiggly" universe of service processes demand the same rigorous approach to quality as do manufacturing processes. Both need to be objectively described, documented, and measured, using statistical tools and proven quality-management techniques. Yet service processes also must be designed to respond quickly and positively to random events.

ACTION STEP

Look at the lists of new concepts on pages 12 and 13. Identify the three that would most benefit your business if you were to implement continuous process improvement.

There is a good deal of talk today about being customer driven. H. Fred Ale says what it really means: just as a skilled gardener needs to learn to see things from the plant's point of view, so do the producers of goods and services need to learn to see things from the customer's point of view. Being customer driven is like having a green thumb. Only by taking the customer's point of view can you learn what customers really need and want.

This chapter discusses the meaning of "customer driven" and defines three primary types of customers.

THE CUSTOMER'S POINT OF VIEW

My green thumb came only as a result of the mistakes I made while learning to see things from the plant's point of view.

H. Fred Ale

2

WHAT IT MEANS TO BE CUSTOMER DRIVEN

Robert Sommer developed his No. 3 Pencil Principle when his office manager in a government agency banned No. 2 pencils in favor of No. 3s on the assumption that No. 3s would last longer. They did last longer. No one used them.

No. 3 Pencil Principle: If it isn't used, it isn't needed.
—Robert Sommer

This anecdote illustrates what we mean by being customer driven. No. 3 pencils may meet all the conformance standards set by a pencil company: they may be exactly the right length and exactly the right hexagonal shape; they may meet the lowest allowances for lead dust and the highest criterion for point endurance. But if people don't like to use them, these standards are irrelevant.

You have to accept that the customer is in charge and sacrifice everything for him. This idea has to be embedded into your mission.

—Percy Barnevik,
CEO of ABB
(Asea Brown Boveri)

It doesn't matter how excellent or superior an organization considers its goods or services to be if they are not what the customer wants or needs. Being customer driven means providing value-added goods, services, and personal experiences that customers find useful, convenient, and delightful. Being customer driven means seeing and feeling things as the customer does. Being customer driven means meeting and exceeding customer expectations.

Standards are important to improving quality, far superior to vague assertions such as: "I know what quality is, but I can't define it." But narrowly focusing on conformance standards often diverts attention from larger concerns, such as customer preferences and perceptions, marketplace conditions, and so on.

CUSTOMER EXPECTATIONS AND THE ORGANIZATION

Taking the customer's point of view is very different from saying, "Let me list the things my customer wants from me." Many organizations have no idea what their customers really want. A few seem not to care. For example, a "doctor knows best" attitude still prevails in some hospitals. This attitude often is shared by the nursing staff ("nurse knows best"), the clerical staff ("admittance clerk knows best"), and others. This patronizing spirit lurks in other service industries, too. Everyone has encountered a supercilious waiter or a rude clerk. The message that customers receive is that the organization does not care about them.

Other organizations do care but miss the mark, even though they spend a lot of time and resources trying to make customers happy. These organizations tend to be preoccupied with their perceptions of what the customer wants. Sometimes this results in a satisfied customer, but very often it does not.

Being customer driven means being a customer of your own organization. To understand the customer's point of view, a chef must eat at his or her own restaurant. By seeing your organization through the eyes of your customers, you can avoid misunderstanding customer expectations.

For example, a national package delivery service, assuming that customers wanted earlier package delivery, put a great deal of effort into shortening delivery times. It turned out that although customers are always glad to receive a delivery as soon as possible, delivery to the correct address was more important to them. The delivery service found that eliminating errors needed to be the first priority in meeting customer expectations.

A process is improved when the customer perceives things to be better than they were before. A customer-driven approach results in improvements that work, that last, and that count.

WHO IS A CUSTOMER?

Many organizations endorse Drucker's dictum but lack the means of moving from concept to practical application. The key is to put yourself in the place of the person who receives process outcomes: the customer.

Copyright, 1995, Boston Globe. Distributed by the Los Angeles Times Syndicate. Reprinted with permission.

> *A customer is the recipient of one or more of a process's specified outcomes.*

From the point of view of people within particular work processes, the question arises: just who is my customer? For people who work in behind-the-scenes processes away from the public, the idea that they are serving

---

T he purpose of any business is to create and keep customers.

—Peter Drucker

customers may be a new one. On the other hand, those working in processes that directly serve the public may not think of the people within the organization as customers. The question "who is my customer?" requires analysis. There is often more than one answer.

PRIMARY CUSTOMERS

Primary customers are the people for whom the organization exists. They are outside the organization. Usually, they purchase the organization's products or services.

The dictionary defines a customer as one who buys. That's one good definition. The passenger of an airline is a customer, and so is the patient in a hospital. The passenger purchases transportation; the patient purchases care. These are primary customers, people for whom the organization exists. Primary customers sometimes are called "end customers" to indicate that they receive the organization's end product or service.

Primary customers are the people for whom the organization exists. They are outside the organization. Usually, they purchase the organization's products or services.

It is important for people within a process to be guided by the expectations of the primary customer in order to stay aligned with the overall goals of the organization. It is sometimes easy to lose sight of the primary customer when you are absorbed in the workings of your own particular process. For example, because the nurses in a managed-care process carry out the doctors' orders, they may think of the doctors as their customers. But if the process is not driven by the needs and expectations of its primary customers—the patients—the quality of the process's outputs is compromised.

Process improvements driven by the primary customer's perception of quality will always advance the organization's business goals.

SECONDARY CUSTOMERS

Secondary customers have a vital interest—often financial—in the organization.

Secondary customers have a vital interest—often financial—in the organization.

Very often an insurance company pays the major part of a hospital bill. Similarly, a travel agent may actually purchase a traveler's airline ticket. The insurance company and travel agent are secondary customers—intermediaries between the primary customers and the organization. The output they receive from the organization is a byproduct of the primary output of the organization. The insurance company is a proxy for the patient, who (usually along with an employer) pays a premium for the service. The travel agent is a distributor—a middle person between the airlines and their passengers.

Both the travel agent and the insurance company are secondary customers; that is, they have a vital interest, often financial, in the organization's success. Secondary customers do not have to be intermediaries, but they must have a stake in the organization. Investors are secondary customers. A hospital's physicians are secondary customers. Banks are secondary customers in the organizations they make loans to. Suppliers of goods or products to the organization are secondary customers, too. They depend on the organization for their business.

INTERNAL CUSTOMERS

A third category of customer is the internal customer. Internal customers are employees or processes of the organization, inside the organization but outside the process being improved. The outputs they receive usually are needed for their own work. Outputs of a process that do not go to an organization's primary customers probably go to the process's internal customers. For instance, the internal customers of a

Internal customers are employees or processes of the organization, inside the organization but outside the process being improved.

DILBERT by Scott Adams

DILBERT reprinted by permission of United Feature Syndicate, Inc.

"schedule patients" process would include employees in the "register patients" process, who need preregistration information, and to employees in the "manage medical records" process, who need a request for a patient's medical chart.

The satisfaction of internal customers contributes to the improved operation of a particular process, which, in turn, improves the organization's relationship with its primary customers. For example, if the "schedule patients" process sends timely, accurate information to the "register patients" process, the patient has a much better chance of being registered efficiently and courteously. Likewise, if the "schedule patients" process sends a prompt request to the "manage medical records" process, the patient's medical record will be waiting at the time of the appointment so that the doctor has the information he or she needs to provide good care.

THE CUSTOMERS OF A PROCESS

Most processes serve more than one kind of customer. For example, the customers of a clinic's "schedule patients" process might be summarized as follows:

CUSTOMERS OF A "SCHEDULE PATIENTS" PROCESS	
Primary Customers	Patients
Secondary Customers	Physicians
Internal Customers	"Register Patients" Process
	"Manage Medical Records" Process

ACTION STEP

Create a chart that identifies all the customers of your process. Be sure to consider all three categories of customers.

The preparatory stages of process improvement can be thought of as intelligent tinkering. Before you can improve a process, you need to understand why it exists and what it does. It is important to document these things, too. Documenting them is a way of saving them and further understanding them.

This chapter will show you how to look for the whys and whats of a process and how to pull these elements together in a clear definition of the process.

INTELLIGENT TINKERING

The first rule of intelligent tinkering is to save all the parts.

Paul Ehrlich

3

DISCOVER AND DEFINE THE PROCESS

Many people probably believe they know it all when it comes to doing their jobs, and maybe they do. But most have yet to learn the whys and whats of the process(es) that are part of their jobs. To discover and define your processes is the first stage in developing a blueprint for meaningful improvement.

It's what you learn after you know it all that counts.

—John Wooden

DISCOVERY: FROM THE CUSTOMER'S POINT OF VIEW

Your workplace and the processes that occur there may be so familiar to you that to talk about "discovering" them may appear superfluous. But making improvements involves seeing your processes in a new way, detached from familiar assumptions.

Customer partnership is the key to success in today's quality and service sensitive marketplace.

—Ron Zemke, President,
Performance Research
Associates, Inc.

To see a process in a new way, in a way relevant to improving it, you need to look at it through the eyes of your customer. The customer's perspective of a process invariably illuminates its whys and whats.

Processes can be defined from a variety of perspectives. Often, no two people will agree on exactly what constitutes a process even when they both are involved in it. But when everyone takes the customer's point of view, everyone looks at the process in the same way and in a way that is relevant to the organization's success. Thus, the customer's perspective provides a single, objective perspective that everyone can use and that works for all the organization's processes.

DEFINITION: PROOF OF YOUR UNDERSTANDING

Looking at your process from the customer's point of view is a way of exploring your process. Once you have explored it, you are ready to define it. Defining your process is proof that you understand what you've explored. If you can give concrete expression to what occurs in the process and why, you understand it.

Defining your process involves documenting its whys and whats. There are eight steps in doing this:

- ◆ Step 1: Write a process purpose statement.
- ◆ Step 2: Assign a process owner.
- ◆ Step 3: Identify the outputs of the process.
- ◆ Step 4: Determine the end of the process.
- ◆ Step 5: Identify the inputs of the process.
- ◆ Step 6: Determine the beginning of the process.
- ◆ Step 7: Name the process.
- ◆ Step 8: Construct a high-level flow chart of the process.

◼ STEP 1: WRITE A PROCESS PURPOSE STATEMENT

The first thing to understand is the fundamental purpose of your process. You need to know why its activities are performed.

The best way to identify the purpose of your process is to write a process purpose statement. Articulating the purpose is a way of truly understanding it, and once it is written down, others will understand it, too. A process purpose statement explains why the process exists in the organization.

A process purpose statement explains why the process exists in the organization.

Following these two rules in writing your process purpose statement will help you to keep it focused and crisp:

◆ Begin with the word "to" followed by a verb. Processes are made up of their activities, and activities can be described only by verbs.

◆ Limit your statement to one or two complete thoughts, expressed in no more than two sentences.

A Summary of Customers and Outputs

One way of looking at a process purpose statement is as a summary of the main customers and outputs of the process. Using an example from health care, and putting yourself in the customer's shoes, as a patient, what output do you expect when you call a clinic? Probably an appointment to see a doctor or receive some other clinic service, such as a laboratory test. A purpose statement for a "schedule patients" process that summarizes its main customers and outputs might be: *To provide patients*

A process purpose statement summarizes the customers and outputs of the process.

with access to clinical resources. Note that the statement begins with "to" followed by a verb. It is a single, complete thought.

A Vision

A process purpose statement expresses a vision of what the process should be in the future.

In addition to summarizing the customers and outputs of a process, a purpose statement should also be a vision statement. It should describe not only the process as it exists now but the way you want it to be in the future.

"The future" varies, depending on the state of the process, but it should be a time frame in which you can achieve some goals. This may be six months for poorly functioning processes that are just being brought under control. It may be two years for processes that already are stable enough for you to create new, value-added services.

Let's look again at the process purpose statement for "schedule patients": *To provide patients with access to clinical resources.* How might this statement be revised to reflect a vision of the future? Again, imagine yourself in the customer's position. You want not just an appointment but an appointment that fits into your own schedule. You want a convenient appointment. A revised purpose statement expressing this might be: *To provide patients with timely, convenient access to clinical resources.*

Shared Values

A process purpose statement reflects the organization's shared values.

Another attribute of a process purpose statement is that it reflects the organization's shared values. In the case of a medical clinic, these might be to provide the best possible care and to do it cost effectively.

On examining the purpose statement, *To provide patients with timely, convenient access to clinical resources,* we can see that it does not include the value of cost effectiveness. Accordingly, we might amend the statement to read: To provide patients with timely, convenient access to clinical resources while ensuring efficient use of resources.

Specific Performance Characteristics

The process purpose statement also should identify specific performance characteristics. These do not have to be detailed, but they should be clear enough so that you know when you have succeeded.

A process purpose statement identifies specific performance characteristics.

Examining our purpose statement again, we can see that "convenient" is a specific performance characteristic. If you were to ask a patient whether or not his appointment was convenient, he would be able to respond specifically by saying yes or no. He could even rank convenience on a scale of 1 (convenient) to 5 (not convenient).

The latter part of our statement, while ensuring efficient use of resources, also describes a specific performance characteristic: efficient use. Efficient use can be evaluated and measured in terms of productivity rates and costs.

Process Limits

For small and medium-sized organizations, the process's limits will be those of the organization. The limits of our "schedule patients" process, for example, would be those of the clinic. In such cases, process limits are usually implicit in the purpose statement.

A process purpose statement indicates the process's limits.

For larger organizations, the limits may have to be defined, perhaps geographically or according to organizational divisions. For example, a process's limits may be defined by its regional operations, e.g., "the Western Division." A process in a large, global organization may be limited to the United States.

Customer Population

A process purpose statement defines the customer population.

The customer population is the customers within the limits of the process. Generally, the process purpose statement refers to primary customers. The primary customers of the "schedule patients" process are the patients of the clinic.

There are other customers of the process, as we discussed in Chapter 2, but they are secondary, and the process purpose statement should focus on the customers who depend on the process's main outputs.

For some processes, a stakeholder or an internal customer may also rely on the process's main outputs. A purpose statement for a hospital's "manage resource utilization" process might be: *To establish and operate a mechanism that encourages appropriate use of organizational resources while meeting payor/patient requirements.* For this

---

Tips for Writing a Process Purpose Statement

Most processes are complex; to describe them simply and clearly may require a good deal of thought and discussion. The development of a process purpose statement is an iterative activity. You will want to refine and revise it as you go along.

You may decide to focus on a piece of your process—a subprocess. For example, a "provide diagnostic support" process would include several kinds of diagnostic subprocesses: X-rays, laboratory tests, and so on. A sample purpose statement for one of these, "provide laboratory services," might be: *To provide accurate, timely, patient-sensitive laboratory services.*

process, the output to the insurance company is as important as the output to the patient. The equality of the primary customer and the stakeholder is reflected in the description of the customer as *payor/patient.*

 ## STEP 2: ASSIGN A PROCESS OWNER

Assigning process ownership is a way to establish leadership and responsibility for process management. It is an important early step in improving processes. A process owner is the individual who coordinates all process activities and is ultimately accountable for process performance. By being accountable for the

A process owner is the person who coordinates all process activities and is ultimately accountable for process performance.

success of the effort, the process owner attains a personal investment in the process improvement and fosters teamwork in others.

A process owner is not the same as a department manager. Department managers tend to think of their departments as occupying squares on the organizational chart. Anything that happens outside a manager's square is not his or her responsibility. Many managers do not think in terms of process or in terms of cutting across departmental lines, and few take the customer's point of view.

A process owner, on the other hand, takes responsibility for a process as defined by the customer. For example, if a patient perceives the beginning of an "admit patients" process to be when he or she and the doctor decide on hospitalization, that is when the process begins. A department manager would probably define the process as beginning when the patient arrives at the hospital. A process owner asks when the process begins and ends for the customer, then takes responsibility for it from beginning to end.

The Process Owner

A process owner should be an executive with the authority to make changes. Lack of executive participation and follow-through is the most common reason for the failure of process-improvement efforts. If executives fail to take active leadership roles, employees will question their commitment and the importance of the improvement efforts.

There are other reasons why process owners should be executives. A process owner needs to be high enough in the organization to develop and implement a plan for improving a process. A process owner has to be able to exert significant influence on changes in policies and procedures that affect the process.

A process owner also is the person with the most resources invested in the process. Very likely, this person is in charge of the process's budget. He or she has authority over more of the process's activities and resources than anyone else and has the most influence over process outcomes. The process owner is the person with the most to lose if the process falters and the most to gain when the process succeeds. He or she is responsible for ensuring that all customers are satisfied.

Responsibilities of the Process Owner

The process owner leads the improvement team in documenting the process, carrying out improvement activities, and providing the

The process owner is the leader of the process-improvement team. He or she is responsible for defining and documenting the process. This includes leading the team in determining the process's outputs, customers, inputs, and suppliers. It also includes helping the team to define and pursue improvement objectives and to establish the measurements and controls to monitor progress. The process owner also oversees the analysis and interpretation of the data. This perspective often requires a paradigm shift.

As the executive in charge, it is up to the process owner to see that the improvement effort has the resources it needs to succeed, in terms of people, finances, and whatever else is necessary. The process owner is also responsible for gaining the support of other departments and for providing periodic reports to the other managers in the organization.

Ultimately, it is the process owner who is responsible for ensuring that the process outputs exceed customer expectations. This is the aim of process improvement: cost effectively meeting and exceeding customer expectations. Thus, the process owner is a key player in advancing the organization's fundamental goal of customer satisfaction.

▍STEP 3: IDENTIFY THE OUTPUTS OF THE PROCESS

We have already defined a process as a series of logically related activities performed to achieve a specific outcome. The "specified outcome" can be thought of as a group of related outputs. Outputs are the products, documents, services, or information generated by the process. Outputs are what the customer receives.

To illustrate how to identify the specific outputs of a process, we will go through this step, output by output, for the "schedule patients" process.

Outputs to Primary Customers

Begin by putting yourself in the primary customer's place. The first output you, as the patient, encounter on calling the appointments desk is a response to your call. What sort of response do you expect? Probably, a prompt, courteous response.

So our first output is: *a prompt, courteous telephone response.*

The next output you want to receive is an appointment with a doctor you have requested or who can provide the skills you need at a time that accommodates your own schedule. The second output is: *a convenient appointment with the appropriate doctor.*

You also need accurate information about insurance and payment requisites so that you can bring the correct information and expected payment to your visit. For instance, you may need to bring your insurance card and a certain percentage of the payment.

If you have been scheduled for a laboratory test, you will also need to have the appropriate test-preparation instructions, for example, the need to fast for twelve hours before the test.

Another output might be logistical information, such as directions to the clinic, where to park, directions to the registration desk, and the time you should arrive (e.g., fifteen minutes before the appointment time to take care of paper work).

A final output covers situations when the clinic must change the appointment. This happens when your doctor is unexpectedly unavailable on the day of your appointment. In such cases, the scheduling personnel must provide you with notification of changes.

Therefore, a list of outputs to the primary customers of a "schedule patients" process might look like the following:

Outputs	Primary Customer
Prompt, courteous telephone response	Patient
Convenient appointment with appropriate doctor	Patient
Insurance and payment requisites	Patient
Test-preparation instructions	Patient
Logistical information	Patient
Notification of changes	Patient

Outputs to Secondary Customers

Now let's consider secondary customers. A secondary customer of a process must receive one or more of its outputs. Although an organization's secondary customers (shareholders, lending institutions, and so on) are also indirectly

> *A secondary customer of a process must receive one or more of its outputs.*

stakeholders of all its processes, they may be too far removed from a process to be considered customers of its outputs. This is the case in a "schedule patients" process. The shareholders of a clinic indirectly benefit from how well the process functions, but they do not depend on any of its outputs. Such shareholders are not listed as secondary customers.

Secondary customers can be important to certain processes, however, as can be illustrated by the "manage resource utilization" process described in Step 1, in which third-party payors were named by the process purpose statement as primary customers. The output that third-party payors want, in this case, is *a bill for appropriate care.* The insurance carriers want a bill that reflects the clinic's effort to avoid unnecessary procedures and excess charges.

Outputs to Internal Customers

Although only a few specific processes number stakeholders among their customers, most processes do have internal customers (employees or processes within the organization but outside the

> *Usually, internal customers depend on one or more of the process's outputs for their own work.*

process being improved). Usually, although not always, internal customers depend on one or more of the process's outputs for their own work.

The next process down the line from yours is a good place to look for internal customers. In the case of a "schedule patients" process, there are two: the "register patients" process and the "manage patient records" process. These two processes need *notification of the visit, notification of cancellations and rescheduled appointments, and complete, accurate patient information.* A list of outputs of the "schedule patients" process to internal customers might look like the following:

Outputs	Internal Customer
Notification of visit	Register patients process Manage patient records process
Notification of cancellations and rescheduled appointments	Register patients process Manage patient records process
Complete, accurate patient information	Register patients process Manage patient records process

▙ STEP 4: DETERMINE THE END OF THE PROCESS

All the activities of a process fall between its beginning and end points. The end point of a process is the extent of its activities.

The End from the Customer's Point of View

The end of a process may be defined differently, depending on who is defining it, so it is very important to take the point of view of the customer. To determine your process's end point, look at your list of outputs. Your process will end with one of them. Then ask: when does the process end for the primary customer?

A primary customer of the "schedule patients" process might answer: "When the scheduling clerk and I agree on an appointment time and I have all the instructions I need for a successful visit." We can generalize this end point in a concise sentence: *The "schedule patients" process ends when an appointment time is agreed on and the patient acknowledges preparation instructions.*

A Continuous Whole

One process's end point is an adjacent process's beginning. In a high-quality organization, the junctures of adjacent processes meet neatly to form a continuous whole. There should be no gaps.

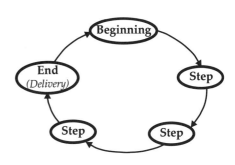

For example, the end point of the "schedule patients" process is the beginning point of the "register patients" process. When an appointment time is agreed on, and the patient acknowledges preparation instructions, an employee in the "schedule patients" process sends notification of the scheduled visit and complete, accurate patient information to his or her internal customer, the "register patients" process. Entering this information into a registration system represents the beginning of the "register patients" process.

A gap between processes can have unfortunate consequences. Take the instance of one hospital's "admit patients" process. The improvement team for this process decided that the process ended with the direction of the patient to the ward. But from the point of view of the ward nurses and the patient, the end point of the "admit patients" process (and the beginning of the "manage care" process) was the arrival of the patient in the ward. In the gap between the two processes, the

"You go across the square, pass the nurse's residence, up the steps, through the main lobby...and second door on your left."

HERMAN© Jim Unger. Reprinted with permission of Universal Press Syndicate. All rights reserved.

patient might become lost, become incapacitated, or be subject to some other random event. This sort of "error" results in a patient's perception of poor–quality care. Such errors can be avoided by making sure that the end point of your process is the beginning of the next process.

To check the validity of your end point, have your customers, both primary and internal, agree on it with you. This will eliminate any gap between your process and the next one.

STEP 5: IDENTIFY THE INPUTS OF THE PROCESS

Your process's inputs are the products, services, or information needed to perform its activities. Think of the inputs needed for a "cut hair" process. One of the most important inputs comes from the customer: hair. As we discussed in Chapter 1, service processes usually require something from the customer to be "processed." The process requires inputs from vendors (e.g., scissors, clippers, combs, shampoos, conditioners, smocks). As this example illustrates, inputs always come from outside the process.

Inputs always come from outside the process. Inputs may, however, come from inside or outside the organization.

Inputs may, however, come from inside or outside the organization. For example, the "issue loans" process in a bank receives validated credit reports for loan approvals from the bank's "provide credit information" process. These reports are inputs from inside the organization but outside the process.

Inputs and Suppliers

To identify a process's inputs and suppliers, first look at your list of outputs. Ask what the process needs from the customer, since customers almost always act as suppliers to service processes. Then ask what your process needs from other suppliers (vendors and other processes within the organization). The "schedule patients" process can be used to illustrate this.

Customers almost always act as suppliers to service processes.

Starting at the top, what do you need from the customer to trigger the output, which is a prompt, courteous, telephone response? The answer is "a request for care." *Request for care is your input.*

OUTPUTS TO PATIENT

Prompt, courteous telephone response

Convenient appointment with appropriate doctor

Insurance and payment requisites

Test-preparation instructions

Logistical information

Notification of changes

OUTPUTS TO INTERNAL CUSTOMERS

Notification of visit

Notification of cancellations and rescheduled appointments

Complete, accurate patient information

What about the next output, convenient appointment with appropriate doctor? Inputs needed from the patient (customer) for this output include *an accurate description of the reason for the visit* (e.g., a check-up request, symptoms if the patient is ill). Other inputs would be the patient's *preferred date and time for a visit* and possibly *the name of a preferred doctor.* In addition to these inputs from the patient, the process also needs an input from the providers: a dependable schedule of what medical skills are available when. The following is a sample table of inputs and outputs for a "schedule patients" process. Note that some outputs do not have a corresponding input and vice versa.

Output	Input	Supplier
Prompt, courteous phone response	Request for care	Patient
Convenient appointment with appropriate doctor	Accurate description of reason for visit	Patient
	Date/time preferences	Patient
	Doctor preference	Patient
	Dependable availability schedule	Providers
Insurance/payment requisites	Insurance information, method of payment	Patient
Test-preparation instructions	Test-preparation instructions	"Provide laboratory services" process
Logistical information		
Notification of changes	Information about changes	Providers
Notification of visit (to internal customers)		
Notification of cancellations and rescheduled appoinments	Timely notifiction of rescheduling	Patient
Complete, accurate patient information	Info. needed by "register patient" and "manage medical records" processes	Patient

◤ STEP 6: DETERMINE THE BEGINNING OF THE PROCESS

Defining the beginning of a process completes the definition of the process's boundaries. Start by looking at your inputs. The beginning will start with one of them. Ask when the process begins for the primary customer. The answer will lead you to the natural beginning.

For a patient of a clinic, the "schedule patients" process begins with a request for care. The description of this might read: *The "schedule patients" process starts when the patient requests care.*

Remember to check your beginning point with your customers to ensure that your beginning matches the end of the process before yours.

STEP 7: NAME THE PROCESS

The name of a department, such as "Accounts Receivable" or "Invoicing," does not describe what is actually done in the process. The work of an "accounts receivable" process is to collect payments; the work of an "invoicing" process is to bill customers.

All processes should be named using a verb-plus-object format.

All processes should be named using a verb-plus-object format. The verb should describe the action—what happens in the process. The object should describe the receiver of the action. "Bill customers" describes the action of the process and the object of the action.

Note that a process is named from the point of view of the people who do the work, not the customer. The name of a process describes its activities, and the perspective of the people who perform the activities is the appropriate one.

Naming your process using the verb-plus-object formula will help you to clarify what really goes on in your process. It will provide a meaningful description of what you do.

▟ STEP 8: CONSTRUCT A HIGH-LEVEL FLOW CHART OF THE PROCESS

A high-level flow chart shows the most important steps in a process from the point of view of the customer. It is not detailed; it consists of only three-to-five blocks. Constructing the high-level flow chart will help you to conceptualize your process and explain it to others.

A high-level flow chart of a "schedule patients" process, from the point of view of the customer, might look like the following:

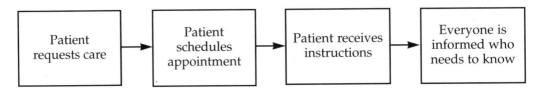

USING THE EIGHT STEPS

When you have completed the foregoing eight steps, you will have defined your process. The sequence described has been found to be useful, but you may want to experiment with it, changing the order slightly if it seems appropriate. For example, some process-improvement teams like to determine their process's beginning immediately after determining its end, temporarily bypassing the identification of inputs. (If you choose this route, check your beginning again after identifying your inputs to be sure it is an input.) The only hard rule is to take the point of view of the customer in all steps except naming the process.

ACTION STEPS

♦ Write a purpose statement for your process.

♦ Assign an owner to your process.

♦ Make a chart of your process's outputs and the customers who receive them.

♦ Complete this sentence for your process: "The process ends when...." Be concise.

♦ Make a table summarizing your process's outputs, inputs, and suppliers.

♦ Complete this sentence for your process: "The process begins when...." Be concise.

♦ Name your process using a verb-plus-object format.

♦ Construct a high-level flow chart of your process from the customer's point of view.

Protozoa are small, and bacteria are small, but viruses are smaller than the both of 'em put together.

Dr. Finagle

To describe protozoa as "small" reflects a subjective, general perception that cannot be verified. One person may assume a protozoan the size of a mosquito. Another may picture a speck of dust. When a protozoan is measured objectively, however, the precise length can be confirmed and is specific enough to be useful.

Similarly, measurements provide objective, specific, and useful information necessary to a process-improvement effort. Measurements furnish data about quantity (how many complaints did your process receive during the last thirty days?), degree (how satisfied are your customers?), and direction (by what percentage have errors been reduced in the past six months?). Measurements provide information that you can use in two important ways: to identify what needs to be improved and to evaluate process performance.

This chapter defines the measurements used to target and track improvements and tells how to establish process-performance measurements for inputs and outputs.

PINNING DOWN THE PROTOZOA

What gets measured gets done.

Tom Peters

4

PROCESS-PERFORMANCE MEASUREMENTS

Measurements are incentives to get things done because they demonstrate unequivocally what needs to be done and how well it is being done now. Measurements provide information that everyone can understand. For example, the number of complaints received in a particular time period is a hard number; it leaves no opportunity for manipulation or wishful thinking.

Measurements quantify perceptions. When a customer complains, "I was put on hold for too long," you can quantify "too long" by tracking the amount of time customers spend on hold. Once you have the measurement data, you can use it to set specific improvement goals. Subsequent measurements will tell you whether or not you are making progress toward those goals.

The professional's grasp of the numbers is a measure of the control he has over the events that the figures represent.

—Harold Geneen,
CEO of IT&T

47

Expressed in specific units, process measurements determine amount (e.g., the number of defects), duration (e.g., the time it takes to do something), and so on. It is important to note that process measurements are applied to the performance of processes, not people.

THE CUSTOMER'S PERCEPTION OF PERFORMANCE

Process-performance measurements quantify the customer's perception of performance.

Using customer-defined performance measurements ensures that your improvements will be relevant to your organization's success.

Process-performance measurements assess a process's inputs and outputs.

Output measurements track how well outputs are meeting customer (internal and external) expectations. For example, a customer survey may reveal that the average amount of time customers expect to wait for their calls to be answered is ten seconds. Monitoring your phone-answering activity will yield data about whether or not this expectation is being met.

Input measurements assess how well inputs are meeting process expectations. For example, grocery checkout clerks need up-to-date, accurate, produce price lists when the store opens each day. Whether this is done can be measured by tracking how many times the list is not delivered by the time the store opens. The number of inaccurate prices provided also can be measured.

HERMAN®

"There goes my tip, right?"

HERMAN © Jim Unger. Reprinted with permission of Universal Press Syndicate. All rights reserved.

Process-performance measurements are objective criteria used to identify areas in need of improvement and to evaluate how well a process works. About 90 percent of all process-performance measurements fall into two categories: cycle time and adverse indicators. The remaining 10 percent can be assigned to an "other" category.

CYCLE TIME

Parkinson's Law is probably one of the best-known tenets of organizational life. It first appeared in 1955 in an unsigned article Parkinson wrote for *The Economist,* and he explained it this way:

> *P*arkinson's Law: Work expands so as to fill the time available for its completion.
>
> — C. Northcote Parkinson

> It is a commonplace observation that work expands so as to fill the time available for its completion. Thus an elderly lady of leisure can spend the entire day in writing and dispatching a postcard to her niece at Bognor Regis. An hour will be spent in finding the postcard, another in hunting for spectacles, half an hour in search for the address....[1]

Parkinson's explanation demonstrates what we mean by "cycle time."

Cycle time is the time elapsed between two specified points in time—the point at which the elderly aunt decides to write a post card and the point at which she puts it in the mail box. Cycle times are measurements that include not just the time spent performing actual work but also the time spent preparing, gathering materials, accommodating interruptions, moving documents around, reworking, inspecting, reviewing, and waiting. Often, the time spent directly generating an output is less than one percent of the process's total cycle time.

Many experts believe that the ideal place to improve quality and performance is by reducing cycle time, which is the total time required to complete a particular process. Steven Hronec, of the consulting firm Arthur Andersen and Company, estimates that most companies that have not tried to reduce their cycle time could reduce it by 80 to 90 percent.[2]

Process Cycle Time

Process cycle time is the total amount of time it takes to receive an output, from the process's start point to its end point. The cycle time for scheduling an appointment with a doctor, for example, is measured from the time you call to request care to the time you acknowledge the appointment time and preparation instructions.

Scheduling health-care appointments is a common task that all of us have experienced. It can be frustrating, even exasperating. We believe that we should be treated as valued customers, but it often seems as if the medical staff is more concerned with accommodating the physicians and the office routines than with acknowledging our needs and meeting our expectations.

Because making an appointment to see a doctor is such a common experience, it is the example used in this book to demonstrate the principles of managing a process from the customer's point of view. The principles involved apply to any manufacturing, service, or administrative processes. An example of the process cycle time for scheduling an appoinment is shown on the following page.

The total cycle time for scheduling an appointment with the doctor is three hours, twenty minutes, thirty-five seconds. Of this time, only eleven minutes, fifteen seconds—or about 6 percent—was spent actually making the appointment. Reducing process cycle time always improves the customer's perception of performance, because customers receive outputs sooner than expected. Reducing cycle time nearly always reduces costs, too, because it often eliminates activities or steps, thereby reducing the number of labor hours, thus requiring less investment per unit of output.

It's important to reduce the right cycle time: the time it takes to receive an output. Once the customer has received the output, he or she wants to take whatever time is necessary for the experience of using the product.

Activity	Elapsed Time
Dial number, wait for four rings.	10 seconds
You are automatically put on hold.	5 minutes
Describe symptoms.	2 minutes
Clerk, unable to assess symptoms, recommends talking to doctor before scheduling appointment. Wait for doctor to call back.	3 hours
Doctor discusses symptoms, recommends a next-day appointment—to include a cholesterol test—and switches your call back to scheduling clerk.	3 minutes
You are accidentally disconnected. Look up number again.	2 minutes
Dial back, wait for four rings.	10 seconds
Wait, as you are automatically put on hold.	2 minutes
Explain that you need next-day appointment and cholesterol test. Negotiate appointment time.	5 minutes
Provide insurance information.	25 seconds
Receive prepayment instructions.	10 seconds
Receive preparatory instructions for cholesterol test.	20 seconds
Acknowledge appointment time and instructions.	20 seconds

For example, if an appointment with the doctor lasts only five minutes, you may believe that you have not received a thorough examination. If a waiter whisks away your entree the moment you put down your fork, you may feel rushed. The cycle time to be shortened is the time a customer spends waiting for the output.

Cycle-Time Segments

Process cycle time can be broken into smaller segments when you want to measure the time it takes to perform a task within the process. In our example of scheduling a doctor's appointment, you might choose to begin with the longest amount of time spent waiting: the time before the doctor called back. You would first track the waiting time over a long enough period (e.g., thirty days) to gather valid baseline data. Then you could set a desirable improvement goal: to reduce the average waiting time for doctor call-backs to thirty minutes. Once you have implemented ways to achieve this, you again track waiting times to see if you are moving toward your goal.

ADVERSE INDICATORS

Give me a fruitful error any time, full of seeds, bursting with its own corrections.

—Vilfredo Pareto

Adverse indicators are the defects, errors, omissions, or unwanted features of outputs and inputs. Adverse indicators measure things that go wrong and things that are missing. They include product defects (e.g., the television set that doesn't work) and defective services (e.g., the repair person who does not arrive as scheduled). "Number of defects" is an important adverse indicator.

Adverse indicators also include other unit-based measurements. A patient who complains that she had to make three separate phone calls to schedule an appointment suggests a useful unit-based measure of the level of bureaucracy that has affected her perception of performance.

Another kind of adverse indicator is the per capita measure. A per capita measure is based on population and is expressed as a percentage. Fifty lost suitcases per 10,000 airline customers is a per capita measure and would be expressed as .5 percent.

Per capita measurements are useful as performance measurements when they measure things the customer sees as a defect, as opposed to a defect that affects the process's efficiency. For example, per capita measurements could be used to determine how many people it takes to move luggage efficiently. Customers do not care about this, although it is a useful internal–control measure. Customers do care, however, that their suitcases are not lost, so per capita measurements relating to this defect are useful as performance measurements. Per capita measurements provide a perspective on how well the process is addressing a given defect or problem. They are useful in assessing the impact of a defect and in guiding the allotment of resources to remedy it.

All these measurements relate to the customer's bad experiences. Bad experiences are powerful determinants of the customer's perception of performance. A traveler's airplane may have arrived safely and on time, but if his luggage was lost or damaged, the customer has a bad experience that can affect his perception of the entire flight. Customers tend to remember what went wrong, not what went right.

Adverse indicators impact customer behavior, too. Very often customers change the way they work with a process after a bad experience. For example, after experiencing the loss of their luggage, many customers refuse to check it in, preferring to carry it on board with them. A mail-order customer may hang up before placing an order when the waiting time is too long. A grocery store customer may decide to shop elsewhere when checkout lines are too long.

Complaints

It sometimes requires a change in mindset to think of adverse indicators as a valuable asset. Errors (adverse indicators) are full of seeds that contain their own corrections.

*W*hen *you have mastered the numbers, you will in fact no longer be reading numbers, any more than you read words when reading books. You will be reading meanings.*

—Harold Geneen,
CEO of IT&T

THE FAR SIDE By GARY LARSON

The Far Side cartoon by Gary Larson is reprinted by permission of Chronicle Features, San Francisco, CA. All rights reserved.

Encourage customer complaints by combining special services and information data gathering. For example, one car dealer offers customers a free ride when they leave their cars for service. During the ride, the driver asks customers what they think of the dealership.[3]

Initially, complaints are probably the best places to look for adverse indicators. Complaints are a rich source of feedback, and an organization needs to examine as many as possible. It may not be so important to reduce the volume of complaints as to change the system to prevent recurrence of the same complaints.

Organizations may need to be educated from the top down in the value of customer complaints. Employees must feel safe forwarding complaints and confident that management wants to hear them.

Once you have the complaints, you may have to do some investigating to determine their true nature. For example, a customer may complain that a service person did not appear at the service desk quickly enough. The complaint may be valid or it may be a substitute for an issue concerning the overall competence of the service department.

Sometimes customers lack the expertise to articulate complaints concerning technical or professional areas. Questioning your customers can yield important information.

"OTHER"

*I*t is necessary to think even to decide what facts to collect.
—Robert Maynard
Hutchins

Not all measurements are cycle times or adverse indicators. Important data may be lost if you do not think of other kinds of useful measurements. Process-performance measurements that are not cycle times or adverse indicators fall into the category of "other."

Customer-satisfaction surveys are probably the most important measurement tools in the "other" category. A valuable means of evaluating outputs, customer surveys yield information that you can translate into measurable characteristics.

Results of customer-satisfaction surveys usually are stated in terms of percent satisfied. Analysis, however, should concentrate on the percent dissatisfied. Concentrating on dissatisfied customers focuses you on what remains to be done. If 92 percent of your customers are satisfied and 8 percent are not, it is the 8 percent that will point the way to a goal of 100 percent satisfied.

Very few processes have mechanisms for monitoring performance in ways that capture customers' value judgments. Customer surveys, spot checks (such as random monitoring of customer-service phone calls), and a complete "manage complaints" process are examples of good feedback mechanisms. Merely establishing a customer feedback loop often results in significant improvements.

"Other" also may include productivity measurements and measurements that are important to secondary customers.

ESTABLISHING PROCESS-PERFORMANCE MEASUREMENTS

Establishing good process-performance measurements will provide you with valuable insight into the performance of your process and will help you to make informed decisions about what to improve. Process-performance measurements are also crucial to assessing progress.

STEP 1: DETERMINE OUTPUT MEASUREMENTS

To determine your output measurements, you first need to identify your customer's expectations: what the customer would like to have and thinks can reasonably be provided. Customers have expectations for every output they receive. Customers expect the basic outputs of a process to have certain characteristics that represent performance or quality to them. A customer expectation usually consists of a noun (the output) and adjectives (the performance characteristics).

To illustrate, consider the outputs you would expect to receive when you call to schedule a visit to the doctor. The first output you expect is a response (noun) to your call. Moreover, you expect that response to be prompt and courteous (adjectives).

The output most important to you is probably the appointment itself. You want to receive an appointment (noun) with an appropriate (adjective) doctor, either the doctor you have requested or one who can provide the skills needed to diagnose and treat your problem. You also want a convenient (adjective) appointment, one that accommodates your schedule.

The table on the following page shows the customer expectations of the "schedule patients" process—the outputs (taken from the chart developed for step 3 in Chapter 3) and their respective performance characteristics.

A good way to develop performance measurements is to look at each performance characteristic and consider which kind of measure—cycle time, adverse indicator, or other—could quantify it. For example, a prompt telephone response requires a cycle-time measure: how many seconds elapse between the time the phone rings at the appointments desk and the time someone answers it.

Ninety-nine percent accuracy in goods or services may sound good, but it results in the following:[4]

♦ At least 20,000 wrong drug prescriptions each year;

♦ Unsafe drinking water almost one hour each month;

♦ No electricity, water, or heat for 8.6 hours each year;

♦ No telephone service or television transmission for nearly ten minutes each week;

♦ Two short or long landings at major airports each day.

A courteous telephone response should be measured the *lack* of a courteous response, which is an adverse indicator. The most immediate source of customer feedback on adverse indicators is complaints. The specific measure here would be the number of complaints about the lack of a courteous response.

Schedule Patients Process
Customers, Outputs, and Performance Characteristics

Customer	Output *(Noun or Noun Phrase)*	Performance Characteristic *(Adjective)*
Patient *(Primary)*	Phone response	Prompt Courteous
Patient *(Primary)*	Appointment with MD	Convenient Appropriate
Patient *(Primary)*	Insurance/ Payment requisites	Complete Accurate
Patient *(Primary)*	Test preparation instructions	Complete Accurate
Patient *(Primary)*	Logistical information	Complete Understandable Accurate
Patient *(Primary)*	Notification of changes	Timely
Register Patients Process *(Internal)* Manage Patient Records Process *(Internal)*	Notification of visit	Timely
Register Patients Process *(Internal)* Manage Patient Records Process *(Internal)*	Notification of cancellations/Rescheduling	Timely
Register Patients Process *(Internal)* Manage Patient Records Process *(Internal)*	Patient information	Complete Accurate

The following table shows the performance characteristics and their respective measurements for the outputs to patients of a "schedule patients" process.

Schedule Patients Process

Performance Characteristics and Measurements for Patient Outputs

Output (Noun or noun phrase)	Characteristic (Adjective)	Cycle Time	Adverse Indicator	Other
Phone response	Prompt Courteous	Time between the phone's first ring and response Time on hold	# of complaints	Customer survey
Appointment with MD	Convenient Appropriate	Time until appointment	# of complaints # of no-shows # of requests for change in MD	Customer survey
Payment requisites Insurance requisites	Accurate Complete Accurate		# of patients without proper payment # of insurance payment denials due to incomplete or erroneous information	
Test preparation instructions	Complete		# of clinically unprepared patients	
Logistical information	Complete Understandable		# of complaints # of late patients and no-shows due to faulty information	Customer survey
Reschedules	Accurate		# of MD-initiated reschedules	
Notification of changes	Minimal Timely	Delay between originally scheduled appt. and new appt.	# of complaints about inconvenience	

The following table shows the performance characteristics and related measurements for the outputs to the
internal customers of a schedule patients process.

Schedule Patients Process
Performance Characteristics and Measurements for Internal Customer Outputs

Output *(Noun or noun phrase)*	Charac- teristic *(Adjective)*	Cycle Time	Adverse Indicator	Other
Notification of visit	Timely	Time between delivery of information and when it is needed		Customer survey
Notification of cancella- tions and rescheduled appointments	Timely	Time between delivery of change infor- mation and when it is needed		Customer survey
Patient information	Complete		# of omissions # of errors	

Recap

To establish your output measurements:

1. List each output as a noun or noun phrase.

2. List every adjective that describes the output in terms of the customer's perception.

3. List every measurement that relates to each adjective.

A good measurement of process performance is specific, objective, easy to understand, and entails practical ways to gather data.

At the beginning, focus on the most important performance measurements. Over time, you can add to your list.

 STEP 2: IDENTIFY INPUT MEASUREMENTS

Very often the first step in improving a process is providing feedback to suppliers about their inputs. Suppliers may have no idea of how their outputs (your inputs) are affecting your process. They may be very willing to make improvements once they understand what needs to be improved. Feedback in the form of objective data is a nonjudgmental way to communicate to suppliers.

To determine performance measurements for inputs, think of your process as a customer of the inputs.

Performance measurements for inputs fall into the same categories as for outputs: cycle time, ad-verse indicators, and other. To determine performance measurements for inputs, think of your process as a customer of the inputs—the products, services, or information that your process needs to perform its activities. What characteristics make a difference in how well your process performs?

To identify characteristics for a schedule patients process, look at the list of inputs developed for step 5 in Chapter 3. For each input, ask if there is a performance characteristic that could be assigned to it. For example, one of the inputs is a description of the reason for the visit. One adjective that expresses a relevant performance characteristic is "accurate." The process needs an accurate description of the reason for the visit.

Not all inputs will have performance characteristics, e.g., "request for care." The "schedule patients" process could not generate its main output without this input, but the performance characteristics of the request are not significant.

The following table for a "schedule patients" process shows the important performance characteristics of its inputs.

Schedule Patients Process
Suppliers, Inputs, and Performance Characteristics

Supplier	Input *(Noun or Noun Phrase)*	Characteristic *(Adjective)*
Patient	Request for care	
Patient	Description of reason for visit	Accurate
Patient	Date/time preferences	
Patient	MD preference	
Patient	Demographic information needed by Register Patient and Manage Medical Records Processes	Complete Accurate
Patient	Insurance information	Accurate
Providers	Availability schedule	Dependable
Providers	Information about changes	Timely
Provide Laboratory Services Process	Preparatory instructions for patient	Complete Accurate
Patient	Notification of reschedule plans	Timely

Each characteristic can be assigned a specific performance measure. For example, the patient's description of the reason for a visit needs to be accurate. How can you measure accuracy? One way might be to track the number of patients who are scheduled with the wrong doctor or wrong medical resource.

The following table includes a column for the specific performance measurements for the inputs of a "schedule patients" process.

Schedule Patient Process
Performance Characteristics and Measurements for Customer Inputs

Input	Charac-teristic	Cycle Time	Adverse Indicator	Other
Request for care				
Description of reason for visit	Accurate		# of misassigned patients	
Date/time preferences				
MD preference				
Insurance information	Accurate		# of errors	
Information needed by Register Patient and Manage Medical Records Processes	Complete Accurate		# of omissions # of errors	
Notification of reschedule plans	Timely	Time between notification of change and scheduled visit		

The following table shows the performance characteristics and related measurements for inputs from the
suppliers of a "schedule patients" process.

Schedule Patients Process
Performance Characteristics and Measurements for Supplier Inputs

Input	Charac-teristic	Cycle Time	Adverse Indicator	Other
Availability schedule	Dependable		# of clinic-initiated reschedules	
Preparatory instructions for patient	Complete Accurate		# of omissions # of errors	
Information about changes	Timely	Time between notification of change and scheduled visit		

ACTION STEPS

♦ Make two tables of your process's outputs (one for your primary customers and one for your internal customers) showing each output's performance characteristics and measurements. Start by referring to your table of outputs developed for step 3 in Chapter 3.

♦ Make a table of your process's suppliers, inputs, performance characteristics, and measurements. Refer to the chart of inputs you developed for step 5 in Chapter 3.

Many organizations fail to achieve significant results from their quality-improvement efforts because they do something described by the Roman philosopher Seneca: they set sail without knowing quite where they are going.

To know where you are going and stay the course requires some navigational tools. You have already defined the key elements of your process in Chapters 3 and 4. This chapter shows you how to put them all together to construct a *Process Profile*® diagram, a "navigational" tool that will help to identify your destination and keep you on course. This is a graphic display of the key elements of your process. It shows what you should be watching as you head toward your goal. It will help you to "catch the right wind."

CATCHING THE RIGHT WIND

When a man does not know what harbor he is
making for, no wind is the right wind.

Seneca

5

PUTTING IT ALL TOGETHER: THE *PROCESS PROFILE*® DIAGRAM*

A *Process Profile*® diagram documents the current state of a process and plans for the future. In navigational terms, it establishes your process's bearings and direction. Its key elements are:

♦ The process's purpose statement

♦ The process owner's name

♦ The process's outputs and their customers

♦ The process's beginning and end

♦ The process's inputs and their suppliers

♦ The process's quality measurements

---

* Reg. U.S. Pat. & Tm. Off. "Process Profile" is a registered trademark of Shaw Resources.

*T*he key is not the "will to win"...everybody has that. It is the will to prepare to win that is important.

—Bobby Knight

These key elements can be expressed graphically to show how they relate. The horizontal arrows show how inputs are acted on by the process to result in outputs, determined by the "expectations" of the process and the customer. The vertical arrows connect a communication channel (horizontal bar) to process elements (circles) to show the continual interaction between what happens within a process and what happens with its outputs and inputs.

Feedback on outputs is used to continually readjust inputs and process activities. Feedback on inputs affects process activities and outputs. The feedback loop works like the governor on a car, which senses engine operations and makes the adjustments necessary for maximum performance.

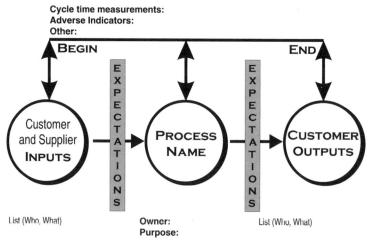

Copyright © Shaw Resources

THE PURPOSE OF A *PROCESS PROFILE*® DIAGRAM

Success requires preparation. Constructing a *Process Profile* diagram is one of the most important preparation tasks for improving a process. A *Process Profile* diagram clearly communicates what a process is, why it exists, and the measurements of quality that will be used to evaluate its performance.

The diagram makes clear what the process improvement team is supposed to work on. Management and the team need to agree on this. Many improvement efforts fail because management directs a team to "go improve something."

The need for management and team agreement about goals is illustrated in the story of a computer company. A process-improvement team decided to improve the company's leasing program, which had been the object of customer complaints. After spending a year revising the program, the proud team made its presentation to executive management. The response was "Why did you do that? Our whole financial plan is based on cash. We can't afford the full-fledged leasing program you're describing."

Constructing a *Process Profile* diagram avoids this kind of conflict. It charters the initial improvement effort by the team, provides a document that delineates the franchise, and sets forth the factors on which to base goals.

A Process Profile® *diagram ensures a shared vision among all relevant parties.*

The *Process Profile* diagram is also a design tool. You can create a diagram to describe a process you are going to build. The diagram acts as your blueprint.

Perhaps the most important function of the *Process Profile* diagram is to ensure a shared vision among all relevant parties—management, team members, customers, and suppliers.

For the team members, working together to develop a *Process Profile* diagram fosters a cooperative spirit. As people gain a clear understanding of their process, they gain confidence in their ability to improve it. For customers and suppliers, the diagram shows how they fit into the process and how important their roles are. For management, a shared vision facilitates clear communication and enlightened leadership.

When everyone shares the vision, choosing and prioritizing what to improve is a cooperative venture. Not only does everyone have a stake in the effort, the objectives are realistic and are related to the organization's purpose.

CONSTRUCTING THE *PROCESS PROFILE*® DIAGRAM STEP BY STEP

Constructing a *Process Profile* diagram involves nine steps. You have already completed the first eight of them in Chapters 3 and 4. To construct a diagram, you transfer the information developed in those chapters to the profile model.

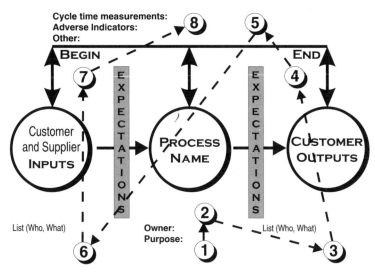

Copyright © Shaw Resources

The steps in constructing the *Process Profile* diagram are as follows:

1. Write a process purpose statement.

2. Assign a process owner.

3. List the process outputs and their customers.

4. Identify the end of the process.

5. List the output quality measurements.

6. List the process inputs and their suppliers.

7. Identify the beginning of the process.

8. List the input quality measurements.

9. Repeat the steps above until no changes are made.

To illustrate, we will construct a *Process Profile* diagram for our "schedule patients" process, going through the steps twice, the first time from the point of view of primary customers and the second time from the point of view of internal customers.

■ STEP 1: WRITE A *PROCESS PURPOSE* STATEMENT

A *Process Purpose* statement describes what the process is supposed to do. It identifies the primary customer and the outputs. The statement for this example would be: *To provide patients with convenient access to clinical resources while ensuring efficient use of resources.*

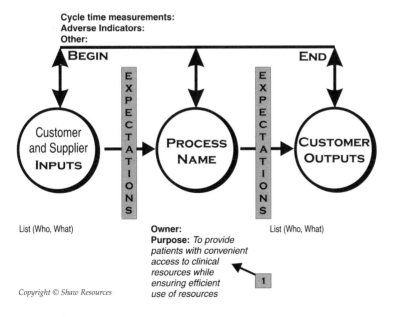

Copyright © Shaw Resources

STEP 2: ASSIGN A PROCESS OWNER

Assigning a process owner ensures accountability. The owner in this example is: *Jane Doe, Executive Director.*

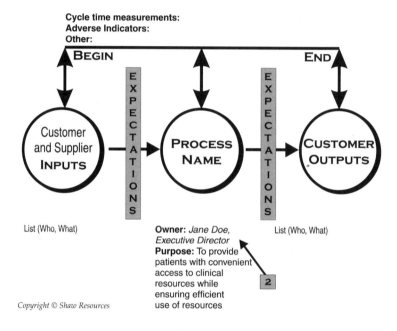

Copyright © Shaw Resources

STEP 3: LIST THE PROCESS OUTPUTS TO THE PRIMARY CUSTOMER

Outputs are products, services, or information generated by the process. The process outputs in this example are: *courteous, prompt phone response; convenient appointment with appropriate MD; logistical information; insurance/payment requisites; test preparation requisites; and notification of changes.* The customers are the *patients.*

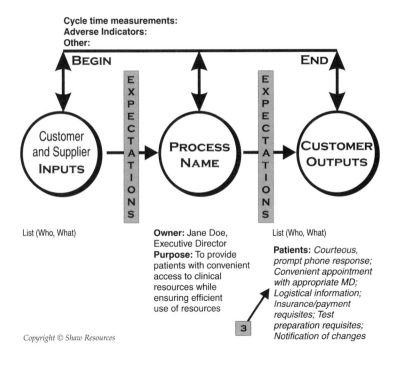

Cycle time measurements:
Adverse Indicators:
Other:

BEGIN   END

Customer and Supplier **INPUTS**

EXPECTATIONS

PROCESS NAME

EXPECTATIONS

CUSTOMER OUTPUTS

List (Who, What)

Owner: Jane Doe, Executive Director
Purpose: To provide patients with convenient access to clinical resources while ensuring efficient use of resources

List (Who, What)

Patients: *Courteous, prompt phone response; Convenient appointment with appropriate MD; Logistical information; Insurance/payment requisites; Test preparation requisites; Notification of changes*

3

Copyright © Shaw Resources

STEP 4: IDENTIFY THE END OF THE PROCESS

Identifying the end of a process answers the question: When does the process end for the primary customer? The end is one half of a process's boundaries. In this example, it is when the *appointment time is agreed on and the patient acknowledges preparation instructions.*

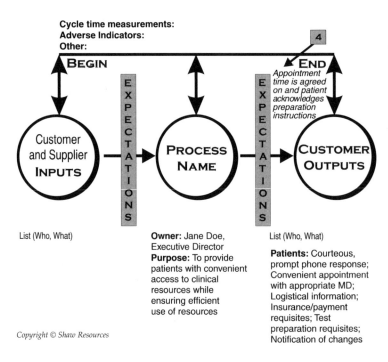

Cycle time measurements:
Adverse Indicators:
Other:

4

BEGIN

END
Appointment time is agreed on and patient acknowledges preparation instructions

E X P E C T A T I O N S

E X P E C T A T I O N S

Customer and Supplier **INPUTS**

PROCESS NAME

CUSTOMER OUTPUTS

List (Who, What)

Owner: Jane Doe, Executive Director
Purpose: To provide patients with convenient access to clinical resources while ensuring efficient use of resources

List (Who, What)

Patients: Courteous, prompt phone response; Convenient appointment with appropriate MD; Logistical information; Insurance/payment requisites; Test preparation requisites; Notification of changes

Copyright © Shaw Resources

STEP 5: LIST THE OUTPUT QUALITY MEASUREMENTS FOR PRIMARY CUSTOMERS

Output quality measurements fall into three categories: cycle times, adverse indicators, and other. Here, cycle time measurements are: _time to schedule appointment, time until appointment,_ and _time to notify of changes._ The adverse indicators are: the _number of complaints, number of requests for change in MD, number of clinically unprepared patients; number of administratively unprepared patients, number of late and no-show patients,_ and _number of clinic-initiated reschedules. Patient satisfaction surveys_ falls in the "other" category.

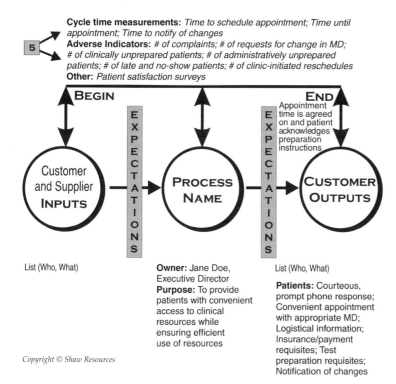

Cycle time measurements: _Time to schedule appointment; Time until appointment; Time to notify of changes_
Adverse Indicators: _# of complaints; # of requests for change in MD; # of clinically unprepared patients; # of administratively unprepared patients; # of late and no-show patients; # of clinic-initiated reschedules_
Other: _Patient satisfaction surveys_

BEGIN

END
Appointment time is agreed on and patient acknowledges preparation instructions

EXPECTATIONS

EXPECTATIONS

Customer and Supplier INPUTS

PROCESS NAME

CUSTOMER OUTPUTS

List (Who, What)

List (Who, What)

Owner: Jane Doe, Executive Director
Purpose: To provide patients with convenient access to clinical resources while ensuring efficient use of resources

Patients: Courteous, prompt phone response; Convenient appointment with appropriate MD; Logistical information; Insurance/payment requisites; Test preparation requisites; Notification of changes

Copyright © Shaw Resources

STEP 6: LIST THE CUSTOMER INPUTS TO THE PROCESS

Customers inputs are the products, services, or information that the process needs from the customer to produce its outputs. In this example, you would list: *request for care; accurate description of reason for visit (symptom); MD preference; date/time preferences; accurate, complete insurance/payment information;* and *timely notification of reschedules* as the inputs. The suppliers are the *patients.*

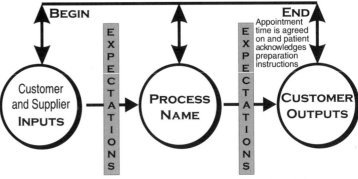

Cycle time measurements: Time to schedule appointment; Time until appointment; Time to notify of changes
Adverse Indicators: # of complaints; # of requests for change in MD; # of clinically unprepared patients; # of administratively unprepared patients; # of late and no-show patients; # of clinic-initiated reschedules
Other: Patient satisfaction surveys

BEGIN

EXPECTATIONS

Customer and Supplier INPUTS

PROCESS NAME

EXPECTATIONS

CUSTOMER OUTPUTS

END
Appointment time is agreed on and patient acknowledges preparation instructions

List (Who, What)

Patients: *Request for care; Accurate description of reason for visit (symptom); MD preference; Date/Time preference; Accurate, complete insurance/payment information; Timely notification of reschedules*

Owner: Jane Doe, Executive Director
Purpose: To provide patients with convenient access to clinical resources while ensuring efficient use of resources

6

List (Who, What)

Patients: Courteous, prompt phone response; Convenient appointment with appropriate MD; Logistical information; Insurance/payment requisites; Test preparation requisites; Notification of changes

Copyright © Shaw Resources

STEP 7: IDENTIFY THE BEGINNING OF THE PROCESS

Identifying a process's beginning answers the question: When does the process start for the primary customer? The beginning is the other part of the process's boundaries. In this example, the process begins when the *patient requests care.*

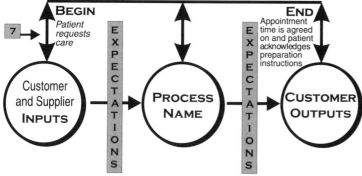

Cycle time measurements: Time to schedule appointment; Time until appointment; Time to notify of changes
Adverse Indicators: # of complaints; # of requests for change in MD; # of clinically unprepared patients; # of administratively unprepared patients; # of late and no-show patients; # of clinic-initiated reschedules
Other: Patient satisfaction surveys

BEGIN
Patient requests care

7

END
Appointment time is agreed on and patient acknowledges preparation instructions

EXPECTATIONS

EXPECTATIONS

Customer and Supplier **INPUTS**

PROCESS NAME

CUSTOMER OUTPUTS

List (Who, What)

Patients: Request for care; Accurate description of reason for visit (symptom); MD preference; Date/Time preference; Accurate, complete insurance/payment information; Timely notification of reschedules

Owner: Jane Doe, Executive Director
Purpose: To provide patients with convenient access to clinical resources while ensuring efficient use of resources

List (Who, What)

Patients: Courteous, prompt phone response; Convenient appointment with appropriate MD; Logistical information; Insurance/payment requisites; Test preparation requisites; Notification of changes

Copyright © Shaw Resources

STEP 8: LIST THE QUALITY MEASUREMENTS FOR CUSTOMER INPUTS

Quality measurements for inputs fall into the same categories as for outputs: cycle times, adverse indicators, and other. For convenience, input and output quality measurements can be merged in your *Process Profile* diagram. Many of the measurements are identical. For example, for the "schedule patients" process, *time to notify of changes* applies to both outputs to customers (internal and external) and inputs *from* customers and suppliers. However, there are two input quality measurements that are different from the output quality measurements: # *of omissions and errors in patient information* and # *of misassigned patients.*

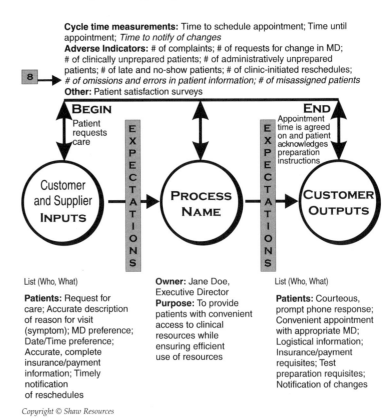

Cycle time measurements: Time to schedule appointment; Time until appointment; *Time to notify of changes*
Adverse Indicators: # of complaints; # of requests for change in MD; # of clinically unprepared patients; # of administratively unprepared patients; # of late and no-show patients; # of clinic-initiated reschedules; *# of omissions and errors in patient information; # of misassigned patients*
Other: Patient satisfaction surveys

BEGIN
Patient requests care

END
Appointment time is agreed on and patient acknowledges preparation instructions

EXPECTATIONS

Customer and Supplier INPUTS

PROCESS NAME

EXPECTATIONS

CUSTOMER OUTPUTS

List (Who, What)

Patients: Request for care; Accurate description of reason for visit (symptom); MD preference; Date/Time preference; Accurate, complete insurance/payment information; Timely notification of reschedules

Owner: Jane Doe, Executive Director
Purpose: To provide patients with convenient access to clinical resources while ensuring efficient use of resources

List (Who, What)

Patients: Courteous, prompt phone response; Convenient appointment with appropriate MD; Logistical information; Insurance/payment requisites; Test preparation requisites; Notification of changes

Copyright © Shaw Resources

STEP 9: REPEAT THE PREVIOUS STEPS FOR INTERNAL CUSTOMERS

STEP 9 - 1: WRITE A PROCESS PURPOSE STATEMENT

No changes; the same as before.

STEP 9 - 2: ASSIGN A PROCESS OWNER

No changes; the same as before.

STEP 9-3: LIST THE PROCESS OUTPUTS TO THE INTERNAL CUSTOMERS

The process outputs in our example are:

> Registration: *notification of visit; complete, accurate patient information;* and *notification of changes.*

> Medical Records: *notification of visit; complete, accurate patient information;* and *notification of changes.*

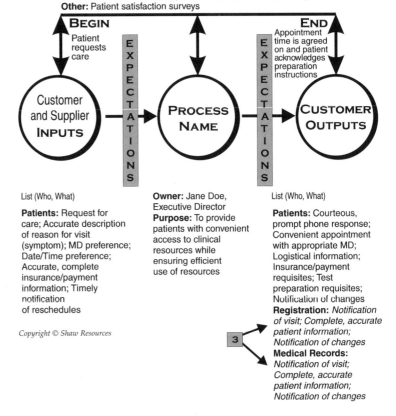

Cycle time measurements: Time to schedule appointment; Time until appointment; Time to notify of changes
Adverse Indicators: # of complaints; # of requests for change in MD; # of clinically unprepared patients; # of administratively unprepared patients; # of late and no-show patients; # of clinic-initiated reschedules; # of omissions and errors in patient information; # of misassigned patients
Other: Patient satisfaction surveys

BEGIN
Patient requests care

END
Appointment time is agreed on and patient acknowledges preparation instructions

EXPECTATIONS

Customer and Supplier INPUTS

EXPECTATIONS

PROCESS NAME

CUSTOMER OUTPUTS

List (Who, What)

Patients: Request for care; Accurate description of reason for visit (symptom); MD preference; Date/Time preference; Accurate, complete insurance/payment information; Timely notification of reschedules

Copyright © Shaw Resources

Owner: Jane Doe, Executive Director
Purpose: To provide patients with convenient access to clinical resources while ensuring efficient use of resources

List (Who, What)

Patients: Courteous, prompt phone response; Convenient appointment with appropriate MD; Logistical information; Insurance/payment requisites; Test preparation requisites; Notification of changes
Registration: *Notification of visit; Complete, accurate patient information; Notification of changes*
Medical Records: *Notification of visit; Complete, accurate patient information; Notification of changes*

3

STEP 9-4: IDENTIFY THE END OF THE PROCESS

No changes; the same as before.

◰ STEP 9 - 5: LIST THE OUTPUT QUALITY MEASUREMENTS FOR INTERNAL CUSTOMERS

The output quality measurements for internal customers are:

Cycle Times: *time to notify of changes; time to deliver patient appointment information.*

Adverse Indicators: # *of omissions and errors in patient information.*

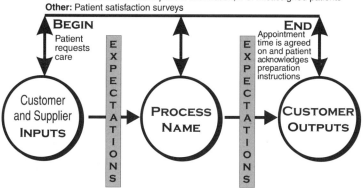

Cycle time measurements: Time to schedule appointment; Time until appointment; *Time to notify of changes; Time to deliver patient appointment information*
Adverse Indicators: # of complaints; # of requests for change in MD; # of clinically unprepared patients; # of administratively unprepared patients; # of late and no-show patients; # of clinic-initiated reschedules; # *of omissions and errors in patient information;* # of misassigned patients
Other: Patient satisfaction surveys

BEGIN
Patient requests care

EXPECTATIONS

END
Appointment time is agreed on and patient acknowledges preparation instructions

EXPECTATIONS

Customer and Supplier **INPUTS**

PROCESS NAME

CUSTOMER OUTPUTS

List (Who, What)

Patients: Request for care; Accurate description of reason for visit (symptom); MD preference; Date/Time preference; Accurate, complete insurance/payment information; Timely notification of reschedules

Copyright © Shaw Resources

Owner: Jane Doe, Executive Director
Purpose: To provide patients with convenient access to clinical resources while ensuring efficient use of resources

List (Who, What)

Patients: Courteous, prompt phone response; Convenient appointment with appropriate MD; Logistical information; Insurance/payment requisites; Test preparation requisites; Notification of changes
Registration: Notification ofvisit; Complete, accurate patient information; Notification of changes
Medical Records: Notification of visit; Complete, accurate patient information; Notification of changes

STEP 9-6: LIST THE SUPPLIER INPUTS TO THE PROCESS

The supplier inputs are:

> MDs: *dependable availability schedule; timely notification of changes.*
>
> Lab: *test preparation instructions.*

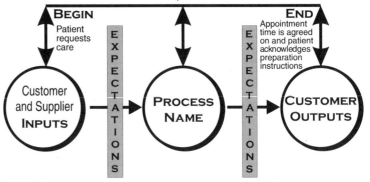

Cycle time measurements: Time to schedule appointment; Time until appointment; Time to notify of changes; Time to deliver patient appointment infomation

Adverse Indicators: # of complaints; # of requests for change in MD; # of clinically unprepared patients; # of administratively unprepared patients; # of late and no-show patients; # of clinic-initiated reschedules; # of omissions and errors in patient information; # of misassigned patients

Other: Patient satisfaction surveys

BEGIN
Patient requests care

EXPECTATIONS

Customer and Supplier INPUTS

PROCESS NAME

EXPECTATIONS

END
Appointment time is agreed on and patient acknowledges preparation instructions

CUSTOMER OUTPUTS

List (Who, What)

Patients: Request for care; Accurate description of reason for visit (symptom); MD preference; Date/Time preference; Accurate, complete insurance/payment information; Timely notification of reschedules
MDs: *Dependable availability schedule; Timely notification of changes*
Lab: *Test preparation instructions*

Owner: Jane Doe, Executive Director
Purpose: To provide patients with convenient access to clinical resources while ensuring efficient use of resources

List (Who, What)

Patients: Courteous, prompt phone response; Convenient appointment with appropriate MD; Logistical information; Insurance/payment requisites; Test preparation requisites; Notification of changes
Registration: Notification ofvisit; Complete, accurate patient information; Notification of changes
Medical Records: Notification of visit; Complete, accurate patient information; Notification of changes

6

Copyright © Shaw Resources

STEP 9-7: IDENTIFY THE BEGINNING OF THE PROCESS

No changes; the same as before.

STEP 9-8: LIST THE QUALITY MEASUREMENTS FOR SUPPLIER INPUTS

The quality measurements for supplier inputs are:

Cycle Times: *time to notify of changes.*

Adverse Indicators: # *of clinic-initiated reschedules, #*
of omissions and errors in test preparation instructions

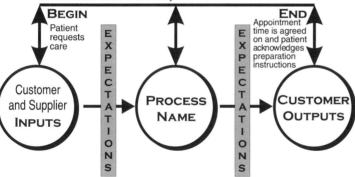

Cycle time measurements: Time to schedule appointment; Time until
appointment; *Time to notify of changes;* Time to deliver patient appointment
infomation
Adverse Indicators: # of complaints, # of requests for change in MD;
# of clinically unprepared patients; # of administratively unprepared
patients; # of late and no-show patients; *# of clinic-initiated reschedules;*
# of omissions and errors in patient information; *# of omissions and errors
in test preparation instructions;* # of misassigned patients
Other: Patient satisfaction surveys

BEGIN
Patient
requests
care

END
Appointment
time is agreed
on and patient
acknowledges
preparation
instructions

EXPECTATIONS

EXPECTATIONS

**Customer
and Supplier
INPUTS**

**PROCESS
NAME**

**CUSTOMER
OUTPUTS**

List (Who, What)

Patients: Request for
care; Accurate description
of reason for visit
(symptom); MD preference;
Date/Time preference;
Accurate, complete
insurance/payment
information; Timely
notification
of reschedules
MDs: Dependable availability
schedule; Timely notification
of changes
Lab: Test preparation
instructions

Copyright © Shaw Resources

Owner: Jane Doe,
Executive Director
Purpose: To provide
patients with convenient
access to clinical
resources while
ensuring efficient
use of resources

List (Who, What)

Patients: Courteous,
prompt phone response;
Convenient appointment
with appropriate MD;
Logistical information;
Insurance/payment
requisites; Test
preparation requisites;
Notification of changes
Registration: Notification
ofvisit; Complete, accurate
patient information;
Notification of changes
Medical Records:
Notification of visit;
Complete, accurate
patient information;
Notification of changes

■ STEP 9-9: REPEAT THE PREVIOUS STEPS
■ UNTIL NO CHANGES ARE MADE

Almost all quality improvement comes via simplification of design, manufacturing, layout, processes and procedures.

—Tom Peters

Constructing a *Process Profile* diagram is an iterative activity. You will want to review each step to correct mistakes, make additions, and clarify what is confusing or vague. Each time you will learn more about your process. You can strengthen your established points and develop new ones.

For example, take the beginning of the "schedule patients" process: *patient requests care.* As time goes on, and you move from meeting customer expectations to exceeding them, you might consider an expanded beginning: *patient decides to request care.* Then you might ask what happens between the time the patient decides to request care and the time he or she dials the clinic number. The patient has to look up the number in the telephone book, for one thing. Is the number listed the proper number to call to schedule an appointment? Is this clear? A proactive approach to the new beginning would be to make it easier for patients to call the clinic. A new output could provide this: a stick-on label with the number of the clinic's appointments desk, a handy list of department phone numbers if the clinic is large, and so on.

Step 9 is a very important one. You will want to make changes until all opportunities to do so have been exhausted and your profile reflects the process as accurately as possible. Later, when changes are made to the process, the same steps can be used to update the model.

ACTION STEP

Construct your *Process Profile* diagram. You can use the diagram below as a starting point. Use the tables and information you developed in Steps 1 through 6 from Chapter 3 and Steps 1 and 2 from Chapter 4.

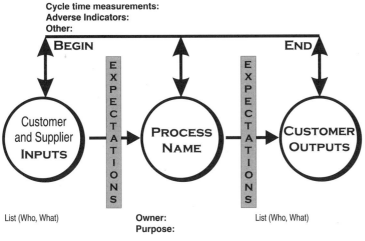

Process Profile Diagram

Copyright © Shaw Resources

*The secret to success is to do the common
things uncommonly well.*

John D. Rockefeller, Jr.

Process improvement is mostly a matter of looking at the common tasks that make up a process and changing how they are done in a way that improves what customers receive. The cumulative impact of numerous common tasks done uncommonly well can result in a world-class process.

This chapter begins by discussing the differences between process improvement and process reengineering and goes on to talk about the process improvement team (PIT), the use of the *Process Profile®* diagram, and the continuous improvement cycle.

Improving the Common Tasks

Process Improvement vs. Reengineering

6

When you arrive at a fork in the road, take it.

Yogi Berra

You are now at a fork in the road. Your *Process Profile* diagram is complete, providing a good picture of what your process does and why. At this point, you have a choice of two roads: process improvement and process reengineering.

Incremental Change vs. Starting Over

Process improvement is a series of incremental changes that accumulate to improve process performance and add value to what customers receive. Reengineering is a starting over, a fundamental rethinking and redesign of a process. Process improvement answers questions such as "How can we do this process faster and more efficiently?" Reengineering answers the question "How can

85

we do this process differently?" Process improvement is gradual and evolutionary, building on what exists. A reengineering effort is a full-scale assault, tearing down what is there in order to rebuild (keeping in mind that you may need to live in the existing structure in the interim).

Process improvement is an ongoing effort, driven by the needs of existing customers. Changes are made to the process in order to meet and exceed customer expectations. For example, Federal Express customers expect their packages to be delivered to the correct addresses. One of the improvements Fed Ex made to meet this expectation was the installation of state-of-the-art sorting equipment to reduce the number of misdirected packages.[1]

Once basic expectations are met, a process-improvement team can generate innovative improvements that surprise and delight customers. Eventually, process improvement serves to change customer expectations, as innovations become the norm. For example, automated teller machines (ATM's) once were innovations. Now people expect banks to offer this service, but they also expect the ATMs to be error-free and available twenty-four hours a day, seven days a week.

Process reengineering is driven by a critical need for operational reform. It is undertaken when the organization needs to meet new demands in the marketplace or is having difficulty competing. Reengineering is chosen when a new way of doing things is needed fast. It is a drastic, once-in-a-blue-moon action.

Reengineering is a drastic action, with attendant high risk, taken when the process is in critical condition. It is a fundamental rethinking and redesign of the process.

The Ford Motor Company, for example, reengineered its accounts payable process in the early 1980s, when slashing costs was crucial to maintaining its competitive position. Ford's old process required five hundred clerks to process three different categories of paper: purchase orders, receiving documents, and invoices. The reengineered process was a radical redesign that dramatically reduced cycle time by eliminating invoices altogether and by integrating and automating purchase orders and receiving procedures. The reengineering team cut 275 employees from the process.[2]

The difference between process improvement and reengineering is like the difference between changing your diet and exercise habits to fight heart disease and having a heart transplant to save your life. The latter entails a much higher risk, but it may be the only choice when time is of the essence. The same is true of reengineering. Reengineering disrupts operations, organizational structures, and employees' lives. Usually, it is used when no other options are available.

HOW TO DECIDE WHICH ROAD

How do you decide which road to take—reengineering or process improvement? It depends on the state of the process and its impact on the organization. A process probably needs to be reengineered when it is critical to the success of the organization and is incapable of producing the needed outputs in the required time.

If you are wondering whether to implement process improvement or a reengineering effort, first ask: Is the process failing to produce the needed outputs in the required time? If the answer is "yes," ask two more questions: Does the process significantly affect the success of the business? Will the organization be seriously damaged during the sometimes lengthy time period required by incremental changes? A "yes" answer to either of these questions indicates that your process may need to be reengineered.

Many reengineering projects have been focused on customer service processes. In the manufacturing sectors, reengineering is aimed at order management and fulfillment, sales, distribution, customer service, and custom product development. In the service sectors, reengineering is undertaken in processes such as underwriting and claims (insurance); royalty management (publishing and entertainment); loan processing (banking and mortgage companies); order management (direct marketing); and customer telephone service (mutual funds and brokerage).[3]

Process Improvement vs. Reengineering		
	Process Improvement	**Reengineering**
Leader	Senior executive or manager working part-time	Full-time senior executive with authority and experience
Team Membership	Cross-functional, cross-level Management, workers, customers, suppliers	Cross-functional, cross-level Management, workers, customers, suppliers
Time Commitment	2-4 hrs per week	Full time
Charter	Make incremental improve-ments to the process	Redesign the process to provide new outputs and/or meet new per-formance requirements
Duration	Forever	Until new process is up and running successfully
Resources	No additional resources Minimal funds allocated as needed	Potentially high investment Precommitted budget
Disruption	Low and gradual	Potentially high
Risk	Low	High
Driver	Customer	Critical need for new function and/or performance
Key Words	Improve	Replace

> Process improvement is for organizations that may be having some health problems; reengineering is for organizations that are in the intensive care ward.

A COMPARISON OF REQUIRED RESOURCES

Reengineering and process-improvement efforts make very different demands on an organization's resources. Because reengineering aims to make a drastic overhaul in a relatively short period of time, it requires a much more substantial, up-front investment than does process improvement. Reengineering requires a large, precommitted budget. If reengineering is the choice, the organization must be prepared to invest significant resources.

Process improvement does not require extra resources. It is funded incrementally, according to the decisions of the executives involved. The costs of process improvement are much lower than those of reengineering.

Reengineering requires a full-time project director. Team members work full time and meet daily.

In contrast, process improvment is carried out by a part-time process-improvement team (PIT), led by a process owner. Once a process has been reengineered, the reengineering team can become a PIT.

THE PROCESS-IMPROVEMENT TEAM

A good deal of theorizing has gone into the subject of improving U.S. business. The best way to improve a business is to improve the business's processes. The best way to improve a process is to examine and improve the "common things" of the process—the tasks that, taken together, form the process.

The best way to examine and improve a process is through teamwork. Teamwork is the key to achieving results that matter in the shortest possible amount of time.

For each process, you need a process-improvement team. PITs are cross-functional and cross-level, led by the process owner, who is ultimately accountable for process performance. A facilitator can manage the group dynamics at first and guide the team through the process-improvement methodology.

Ideally, a process-improvement team comprises 25 percent customers, 25 percent suppliers, and 50 percent people working within the process. Both workers and management should be on the team. Workers bring indispensable knowledge and they, more than anyone, understand process transactions. Because the team will be implementing solutions, not just making recommendations, management representation contributes the necessary authority to make decisions. The team requires enough resident authority to carry out the targeted improvement activities without having to go through a clumsy approval process.

THE *PROCESS PROFILE*® DIAGRAM

The team uses the *Process Profile* diagram as a map. The *Process Profile* diagram guides the team's decisions about what to improve, what data to gather, and what changes to make. The team makes changes in the following three general areas:

Inputs. The process's inputs are improved so that errors and defects will not enter the process and cause problems downstream.

Process activities. The process's internal activities are improved in order to bring the process under control and make it run better.

Outputs. The process's outputs are improved in order to meet and exceed customer expectations. This is the goal. Improving an input often will directly improve an output. Making changes to a process's internal activities is a way of improving outputs, too. Activities focused on improving outputs deal specifically with cycle times, adverse indicators, and other customer-determined process performance measurements.

THE IMPORTANCE OF MIDDLE MANAGEMENT BUY-IN

In emphasizing the role of workers, many continuous improvement programs exclude middle management by default. Left out of the loop and faced with periodically losing effective workers while still being expected to meet productivity goals, the middle manager is not likely to be very supportive of the improvement effort. Some managers have been known to undermine improvement efforts in order to get their staff members focused back "on the job."

*The support of middle management is
essential to the team's success.*

It is imperative to explain to team members' managers why these employees will not be on the job for an hour and a half each week and why they sometimes may be working on assignments in between team meetings. Usually, an overview of what the team will be doing and a request for the manager's support is sufficient. Explain, don't promote. Simply informing managers that the team will be gathering data aimed at improving a process may be all that is needed at first. You may want to invite the managers to the team meetings for awhile, until they decide it is not necessary.

Some middle managers will need to be on the process-improvement team. Managers need to be included when necessary for implementing changes in the process.

THE IMPORTANCE OF EXECUTIVE SUPPORT

The participation of key executives is important in the launch of a process-improvement initiative. The CEO, COO, or another high-ranking executive should be present at the kickoff meeting. Invite the process owners of other processes at equivalent levels, too. The attendance of top brass serves two functions. First, their appearance shows the team just how important management considers quality improvement to be, and it impresses on the team the significance of what they will be doing. Second, attending the meeting is a way for executives to become acquainted with the people on whom they are relying to make improvements.

*We, the senior managers, are
the biggest problem [in improving productivity]. We assume too
much; like our powers too much.*
—Robert Galvin, CEO,
Motorola Corporation

THE CONTINUOUS-IMPROVEMENT CYCLE

The work of the process-improvement team is a never-ending cycle. In general, the four steps proceed as follows:

1.   *Select an improvement opportunity.* The team examines the issues and chooses one process to improve.

2.   *Analyze the process.* The team gathers and analyzes data about the process relevant to the opportunity.

3.   *Change the process.* The team pilots and makes changes aimed at improving the selected issue.

4.   *Review results.* With the changes in place, the team measures process performance and compares the results to performance before the improvements were made.

Continuous-Improvement Cycle

What makes the improvement cycle continuous is the conviction that a process always can be improved. The team repeats the four steps of the improvement cycle over and over. With each cycle, quality improves and quality consciousness rises. With improved quality and quality consciousness come new improvement opportunities. The cycle continues.

TIP

♦ When selecting team members, first identify the titles and positions that should be represented on the team. When that is done, you can begin to identify specific individuals.

When eating an elephant, take one bite at a time.

General Creighton W. Abrams

Improving the quality of processes is a very large undertaking. It can be overwhelming unless you take it in stages. Qualifying a process is like eating an elephant: it is best done one bite at a time.

This chapter defines six stages, or levels, of process performance. Each level consists of a number of improvement activities that, when completed, qualify a process for that specific level.

How to Eat an Elephant

Between vague wavering Capability and fixed indubitable Performance, what a difference!

Thomas Carlyle

7

Process Qualification

A process qualification system gets down to the brass tacks of performance. Process qualification is a formal method of evaluating and ranking a process's performance. It applies objective standards to performance so that everyone has a common understanding of the process's level of performance. This lets management know what to expect from the process-improvement team and lets the process-improvement team know what to aim for. Process qualification is also motivating, because it provides milestones and recognition points that demonstrate the progress of the process and that encourage and reward people for their efforts.

A Definition of Performance Levels

The following chart defines six "performance levels" of processes.

Level	Status	Description
6	Unknown	Process status has not been determined. All processes are classified at this level until sufficient data have been collected to determine their true status.
5	Defined	The process design is understood by the team, and key aspects are documented. It meets the most important operational requirements, and its performance is being measured from the primary customer's perspective.
4	Functional	The process meets all requirements for level 5. Primary customer expectations are being met. The process is systematically measured, and streamlining has started.
3	Proficient	The process meets all requirements for level 4. The process's cycle time, defects, cost of quality, and operational costs are being reduced. The process is efficient, and cost savings are substantial.
2	Premier	The process meets all requirements for level 3. Outputs have been error free for at least six months. Schedules are always met. Worker stress levels are low.
1	World-Class	The process meets all requirements for level 2. The process is rated among the top 10 percent of its kind in the world and is frequently benchmarked by others.

CHECKLISTS FOR PROCESS QUALIFICATION LEVELS

First Law of Wing-Walking: Never leave hold of what you've got until you've got hold of something else.

—Donald Herzberg

Qualifying a process is not as dangerous as wing-walking, but the principle from the early days of barnstorming applies here. Each qualification level is something to "hang on to" before the team can confidently move on to the next level.

To qualify for a certain level of performance, all the activities belonging to it must be completed by the team and validated by a "Process Improvement Council" or its equivalent. Once a process has qualified for one level, the team begins work on the activities of the next level as part of the continuous improvement effort.

The following charts provide brief explanations of the improvement activities belonging to levels 5 and 4, the levels most processes achieve in the first two years or so of a process-improvement effort. A summary of activities belonging to levels 3 through 1 also is provided.

☑ LEVEL 6: UNKNOWN

The status of the process has not been determined. All processes are classified at this level until sufficient data have been collected to determine their true status.

☑ LEVEL 5: DEFINED

The process design is understood by the team, and key aspects of the process are documented. The process meets the most important operational requirements, and its performance is being measured from the perspective of the primary customer.

Checklist Items

Process ownership has been assigned. The process owner, preferably an executive, is the person with the most resources invested in the process and whose performance evaluation depends, in part, on the process's improvement.

Team membership has been established. Roughly half the members of the team should be people who do the work of the process, and the other half should be customers and suppliers. Where it is not possible to include external customers, the members of the team who are charged with collecting data from them can serve as their representatives.

Support from middle managers has been pledged. Middle managers who have employees who work on the improvement team need to understand and support the improvement effort.

Checklist Items

All customers have been identified. There are three main categories of customers:

> *Primary customers* are outside the organization. Usually, they purchase the organization's products or services.
> *Secondary customers* are people who have a vital interest, often financial, in the organization.
> *Internal customers* are employees or processes within the organization but outside the process being improved.

Customer expectations, which include the process's outputs and the adjectives that describe them, have been indentified, validated, and documented. Customer expectations are what the customer would like to have and thinks reasonably can be provided. For example, a customer entering a fast-food restaurant and a customer entering a five-star restaurant use different adjectives to describe the kinds of meals they expect. The output step of the *Process Profile®* diagram identifies the basic outputs and some of their characteristics, which can be validated by benchmarking, monitoring customer behavior, and recording complaints.

Measurements that reflect the customer's view of the process are identified; quality measurements are set; and systems to collect the data are established.

Customer quality measurements can be categorized as follows:
> *Cycle time* is time elapsed between two points, such as the time it takes to generate an output. Reducing cycle time without compromising other quality measurements will always result in an improvement.
> *Adverse indicators*—defects, errors, or unwanted features—can be powerful determinants for customers.
> *Other:* Measurements not easily categorized as cycle time or adverse indicators fall into this category. They can be identified through customer surveys, focus groups, and other feedback techniques.

Improvement objectives for the customer's three most important quality measurements have been defined and are being pursued actively. Objectives should be SMART: specific, measurable, achievable, repeatable, and time related.

Inputs and their related requirements and quality measurements have been identified, and data are being collected. What are the inputs? From whom are they received? What are the input requirements, as defined by the process? What are the quality measurements that you use to judge inputs? How are the data being collected? Completing the steps related to the input side of the *Process Profile®* diagram usually satisfies this item.

Checklist Items

The end of the process has been identified and agreed on with all customers, and the beginning of the process has been identified and agreed on with all suppliers. Customers and suppliers are outside, yet vitally related to, the process. They need to confirm the process's boundaries so that no gaps exist between the organization's processes. If processes were members of a relay team, a gap between them would result in a dropped baton. In the case of processes, however, it is the customer who is dropped.

A high-level flow chart of the process—from the customer's point of view—has been completed. This flow chart helps the team to understand the process as it works now from the customer's point of view. The flow chart also can be used to explain the process to people outside the team. Often, the team's first flow chart takes the process workers' operational point of view. This is a natural starting point, but it needs to evolve into a flow chart that reflects the customer's point of view before this item can be checked off.

Measurement charts of process performance have been posted where they can be seen by staff members and they are updated regularly. This is a way of providing feedback to the people who do the work. Most people want to do a good job, but they need feedback. Otherwise they have no idea whether or not they are doing the right thing, or whether they could change to improve process outputs.

Control points have been defined, and measurements indicate that the process is stable and meets the most important customer expectations. *Control points* are places in the process to take measurements in order to verify that the process is doing what it is supposed to do. A control point is often the place where an activity is completed or where accountability changes. Good control points may be major decision blocks on the flow chart, places where complaints end up, or places where events signifying that something is wrong occur. (An example of the latter is the place a patient calls to inquire about an overdue report on test results.)

Cost data are being collected, and the cost of one process activity has been estimated. List the steps involved and estimate the costs associated with each step.

A review process has been established and is scheduled to be conducted at least every six months. Regular reviews are checkpoints for the team and management.

LEVEL 4: FUNCTIONAL

The process meets primary customer expectations. It is systematically measured, and streamlining has started. Obvious errors have been corrected, and some cycle times are probably shorter, but significant cost savings have not yet begun. The following checklists summarize the activities that need to be completed for levels 3 through 1.

Checklist Items

All requirements for level 5 have been met. This item cannot be checked off until all items for level 5 have been fulfilled. Level 4 achievements cannot be substituted for unfulfilled level 5 requirements.

A flow chart has been created of the overall process as it currently exists, and it has been documented from the customer's point of view. Documentation includes quality measures, control points, and key operational steps. Things that are not working well should be identified. Documentation should be simple, understandable, and organized so that it can be updated over time.

Data are being collected on process cycle time, cost per cycle, and other efficiency measurements. Very often the act of collecting and analyzing data increases awareness of what needs to be improved. Efficiency measurements help assess the costs of resources consumed per unit of work.

Substantial improvement activities aimed at streamlining the process are in progress. The most obvious steps in reducing the number of activities and in shortening the cycle times of the process have been taken. Less obvious steps have been identified and prioritized for action. A list of action items, the people responsible for them, and dates for their completion has been created. The measurements show a trend toward a rise in quality.

Overall operational requirements have been met. Operational requirements focus on key internal measures and controls such as audit trails, and timeliness and accuracy targets. Operational requirements often are established for a complex process's major subprocesses. For example, a "collect payments" process might have an operational requirement that two people count and sign for money received.

Checklist Items

Internal improvement objectives are 50 percent accomplished, and the results have been posted. These objectives reflect an internal view of operations and aim to eliminate errors before they impact the customer. This internal target is intended to improve the process's effectiveness.

"Challenge objectives" that are important to customers have been established and are being pursued. Challenge objectives are external objectives that are established once special variations have been eliminated, defects are within control limits, and the most important customer expectations are being met. Challenge objectives reflect what is important to the customer, and what the process could be doing but currently isn't. These objectives are defined in terms of the process measurements: cycle time, adverse indicators, and other performance measurements.

Customer feedback measures established for level 5 confirm that customer expectations are being met. Sometimes an organization may decide not to meet a customer expectation because it would be too expensive, it would be beyond the organization's capabilities, or for some other reason. In these cases, the organization needs to _establish_ and _manage_ new customer expectations.

Benchmarking has started. Team members have contacted organizations similar to theirs to determine benchmarking criteria. "Best practices" are being identified.

Measurements of the four "cost of quality" factors have been developed, "cost of quality" has been computed, and trends have been identified. The four "cost of quality" factors are:

1. _Internal failures_ are defects discovered before the product or service reaches the customer.

2. _External failures_ are defects discovered by the customer.

3. _Appraisal_ refers to inspection activities, undertaken to prevent internal failures from becoming external failures.

4. _Prevention_ refers to activities undertaken to change the system so that a defect is eliminated or never occurs in the first place.

The formula for computing the "cost of quality" is to add the costs of the first three factors and subtract the fourth. The cost of quality is then weighed against the benefits of quality. The prevention of a defect or fixing it after discovery may be more costly than living with it.

Checklist Items

Formal job procedures exist, and employee training is being conducted.

The improvement team understands and uses statistical process control (SPC). Team members often need to know how to use the "run control" and bar charts that result from SPC.

Tracking and analysis of customer complaints have begun, and results have been posted. Organizations sometimes punish workers rather than reward them for reporting complaints. Workers must feel safe when reporting complaints and feel confident that management wants to hear them. They should be given feedback about the resolution of complaints.

LEVEL 3: PROFICIENT

The process's cycle times, defects, costs of quality, and operational costs are being reduced, resulting in an efficient process. Cost savings are substantial at this level, because scrap and rework have been cut so that output requires fewer resources. Customers are receiving all the required and expected outputs.

❏ All requirements for level 4 have been met.

❏ The cost of defects is being reduced.

❏ Cycle times, operational costs, and bureaucracy are being reduced.

❏ Most quality measurements show improvement.

❏ Crucial suppliers meet process requirements for inputs.

❏ The documentation of subprocesses has been completed.

❏ Workers are being formally trained in team methods and problem-solving tools.

❑ All employees involved in the process understand the *Process Profile®* diagram.

❑ Customer expectations have been benchmarked.

❑ Plans exist to formally benchmark the process.

❑ A proactive customer-satisfaction measurement system has been established that includes capturing 100 percent of all customer complaints.

❑ The customer reviews process changes before they are implemented.

❑ Customer desires have been identified, and plans to meet them have been created.

❑ Statistical process control (SPC) training needs have been identified, addressed, and implemented.

❑ All suppliers have committed to improving the quality of inputs to the process.

✓ LEVEL 2: PREMIER

Outputs have been error free for at least six months. Rarely is there a problem in the process, and stress levels are low. The organization continues to improve. The focus has moved from fundamental goals such as cost savings to critical goals such as accident prevention and strategic goals such as gaining market share.

❑ All requirements for level 3 have been met.

❑ Output schedules have been met without fail for at least six months.

❑ Customer expectations consistently have been met for the last six months or more.

❑ Customers attend process-performance reviews.

❑ Customer expectations are updated regularly.

❑ Customers' desires are being met.

❑ Ways to delight the customer have been identified.

❑ Run control charts are used regularly.

❑ Feedback systems have been established close to the work they concern.

❑ The people who do the work also perform most of the related measurements.

❑ All measurements show improvement during the last six months.

❑ An independent audit plan has been developed and is being used.

❑ Documentation is updated regularly.

❑ All employees have been trained in statistical quality control (SQC) as it applies to their job requirements, and they are scheduled for a refresher course.

❑ Employees evaluate the job-skill training positively.

❑ The process has been formally benchmarked, and objectives have been established.

❑ Employees are empowered to provide help to customers and are measured accordingly.

❑ Employee surveys substantiate that the process is easier to use.

❑ A philosophy exists that errors are unacceptable.

❑ Everyone works tirelessly to prevent errors.

LEVEL 1: WORLD-CLASS

The process is world-class, in the top 10 percent of like processes in the world, and continues to improve. Companies you respect and could benchmark are your equals. If a Malcolm Baldrige or Deming Award winner were to come to you to ask how you do it, you would be able to teach the methods that could be used to improve.

- ❑ All the requirements for level 2 have been met.
- ❑ No customer has complained about unmet expectations during the past six months.
- ❑ Many customer desires are met.
- ❑ Customers are delighted by innovative products or services.
- ❑ All measurements have exceeded those of the benchmark for three consecutive months.
- ❑ The process often is benchmarked by others in the industry.
- ❑ All supplier inputs meet requirements.
- ❑ Employees are regularly surveyed to identify additional improvement possibilities and training needs. Their suggestions are acted on.
- ❑ The process handles exceptions better than the benchmark process does. Exceptions are documented and tracked.
- ❑ World-class status is confirmed by an independent audit.

PROCESS QUALIFICATION AS A PLANNING TOOL

To guide any sort of endeavor successfully, you need to know two things at once:

- ♦ Where you are
- ♦ Where you are going

We must ask where we are and whither we are tending.
—Abraham Lincoln

The process-qualification-level (PQL) system can help you in this. In addition to providing a way to evaluate the performance of processes, the PQL system also serves as a planning tool for both management and teams.

A PLANNING TOOL FOR MANAGEMENT

A process qualification system is a useful planning tool for management because it codifies the status of all the organization's processes, providing an overview of each process's relative status. A simple chart can show which processes need attention. For example, the following chart shows that the "manage complaints" process has advanced to level 5 and the "collect payments" process has advanced to level 4, while the "obtain orders" and "fill orders" processes are at level 6. Management can see at glance that the "obtain orders" and "fill orders" processes need the most work.

Process	Level					
	6	5	4	3	2	1
Manage Complaints		X				
Collect Payments			X			
Obtain Orders	X					
Fill Orders	X					

A PLANNING TOOL FOR THE TEAM

Since the PQL checklist sets out all the improvement activities required by a targeted performance level, teams can use it as a road map. Once a team has investigated the current condition and established some initial objectives, it is ready to work on qualifying the process at performance level 5. The team goes through the checklist for level 5, item by item, checking off completed items, determining the status of others, and assigning uncompleted items to team members as action items.

*A process has qualified for its targeted
level when all its linked activities have
been validated as complete.*

Sometimes a team will complete most of the activities of one level and some of the activities of the next level. In this case, the process has not qualified for either level. Process qualification evaluates the complete process.

TIPS

♦ Allow enough time for a team to qualify its process. Times will vary from organization to organization, but it is not unusual for a team to require four to six months or more to achieve level 5. Level 4 may require at least eight additional months.

♦ All processes in the organization may not need to reach the highest levels. Level 1 (world-class) can be costly and unnecessary for many processes. Initially, it may be best to bring all key processes up to level 4 (functional). Once the key processes are under control, the organization can choose which ones to bring up to level 3 or level 2.

First Law of Electrical Appliances:
They work better if you plug them in.

Anonymous

Process improvement teams are like electrical appliances: they work better when you plug them in to the organization. Reviewing process improvement with management is a way to do that. Regularly scheduled reviews keep management connected to the work of the team and provide management with an opportunity to recognize the team's achievements. At the same time, the team can hear about management's concerns and the larger picture. Regularly conducted process-improvement reviews are energizing; they remind the team of past accomplishments and future plans and they strengthen management's support.

This chapter discusses the importance and benefits of regularly conducted process-improvement reviews and what to include in them.

PLUGGING IN

8

Business will be better or worse.

Calvin Coolidge

THE IMPORTANCE OF PROCESS-PERFORMANCE REVIEWS

Like business, processes either get better or worse. They do not stand still. If they are not continuously improved, they degrade. Conducting reviews at regular intervals is a disciplined way for both management and the team to assess the process-improvement effort and keep it on track.

The most important thing about conducting process-performance reviews is to make them happen. It is easy to postpone them because of busy schedules and the press of everyday operations. But time and again, improvement efforts begin to fall apart when reviews are not

Make no mistake: realizing significant improvements in the quality of a product or service...is hard, hard work involving a serious amount of grunting and sweating and heavy lifting on the part of all employees.

—John Guaspari

109

conducted at regular intervals. Like any other strategic goal, process improvement needs to be watched and nurtured.

Four good reasons to conduct reviews regularly are as follows:

- ◆ *To evaluate the process's performance.* Everyone needs to have an objective measure of how well the process is doing.

- ◆ *To give management an understanding of what is being improved.* In reviewing the team's work, management obtains a better understanding of the workings of the process, customer expectations, and so on. Also, by reviewing all teams, management gains an overall picture of the organization's process-improvement efforts.

- ◆ *To give the team a chance to look at all it has achieved and to be recognized for its efforts.* After five months or so, a team may lose sight of how much good it has done. The team may be unaware of the cumulative impact of the many small steps it has taken. Team members may feel burned out. Seeing what they have achieved revitalizes them.

- ◆ *To plan for the future.* The team sets future objectives and process-qualification-level (PQL) goals, while management assesses them in the context of the organization's goals and strategies.

For teams that are meeting weekly and making substantial improvements, reviews should be held every six months. For teams that are meeting every other week and making small improvements to a stable process, a review every nine months is probably sufficient.

THE REVIEW PRESENTATION

The review presentation planned by the team members should be as simple as possible, yet contain everything everyone needs to know about the state of the process. A review presentation provides people with the information they need to make good decisions for the organization. Senior management can learn about day-to-day staff problems and obtain the information it needs to allocate resources and guide the organization's quality-improvement efforts. Staff people can learn about the organization-wide concerns of management, how their processes fit into the organization as a whole, and other information that helps them to decide what changes to make to their processes.

> *E*verything should be made as simple as possible, but not simpler.
>
> —Albert Einstein

THE REVIEWERS

The reviewers will most likely be the executives who chartered the team—a "process improvement council" or similar body. Generally, but not always, the reviewing body is made up of peers of the process owner, some of whom may be process owners themselves. Sometimes key customers and suppliers are included.

Reviewers are not just judges and information gatherers. They are participants in the review, helping the team to move ahead and making sure that the team's plans plug into the organization's strategic objectives. The role of management is not only to keep track of the team's progress but also to help the team succeed.

It might help for the reviewers to think of the team as their customer. They may even want to conduct an informal review of the review by asking team members what they found valuable and what they did not.

Six Ways to Empower Employees for Quality Improvement:[1]

1. Involve employees in developing strategies for continuous improvement.

2. Provide employees with the skills required to solve problems and make decisions.

3. Define involvement and empowerment based on the mission of the organization.

4. Establish organizational and individual goals.

5. Establish customer-driven performance measurement at the individual level.

6. Involve and empower everyone to focus on continuous improvement.

WHAT TO INCLUDE

The objective of a review presentation is to show management the work that has been completed and the work in progress and to describe the work that is planned for the next six months.

A review presentation usually includes the following:

Process Profile®. Presenting the *Process Profile* diagram at the beginning of the review provides an opportunity to highlight changes and explain how and why they were made. For example, the team may have indentified new customers or suppliers. It may have expanded the scope of the process's purpose. It may have discovered additional adverse indicators or identified other process-performance measurements. Team membership also may have changed.

After team members (or the process owner) have explained the changes in the *Process Profile* diagram, the reviewers validate them. It is important that everyone agree on the process's purpose, the beginning and end of the process, suppliers and inputs, customers and outputs, and quality measurements. This is the common ground of the review.

Key Activities. The specifics of this topic vary from team to team. They also depend on whether it is the team's first review or the tenth. For example, a team's first presentation might describe discoveries the team has made about the process and quick fixes. The team probably will display data collected about issues, customer expectations, and defects. As time goes on, and the team becomes more customer oriented, key activities are likely to shift from what the team is learning about the process to what the team is learning about the customers. Before each review, the team members reflect on their activities of the past six months and decide what is important for management to know.

© Tony Stone Images

Preparing for a review is a matter of selecting and organizing the team's existing documentation.

Customer Feedback. The team's efforts in collecting customer feedback deserve special emphasis. Very often this information is new to management, but it is as important to management as it is to the team. Team members will talk about what they've learned from observing customer behavior, customer complaints, compliments, inquiries, customer surveys, focus group results, or any other form of customer feedback. This is a chance to demonstrate the customer focus of process improvement.

Status of Past Objectives (from the second review on). The team prepares a report on what it has done to meet the objectives (usually three) announced at the last review. Team members explain the improvements they have made and present the relevant data. For example, if one objective was to reduce the number of medical-claims rejections by 50 percent within ninety days, the team might show the steps it took to reduce errors in recording patients' insurance information. Then they might show a run chart that displays the decline in rejections.

N*o one can be the best at everything. But when all of us combine our talents, we can be the best at virtually anything.*

—Don Ward

New Objectives. The team presents its new objectives (usually three) for confirmation by the reviewers.

The team explains why the objectives were selected and how they fit into the overall improvement plan, and the reviewers ask any necessary questions. This is a good opportunity for the team to be exposed to management perspectives and to gain a sense of the organization's overall goals.

Benchmark Information. As the team begins to make changes to its process, it can use informal benchmarking to see how other organizations perform the same process. Later on, the team should undertake a formal benchmarking activity aimed at investigating the best practices in the industry. As part of the review presentation, the team describes the organizations that have been benchmarked and explains why they were chosen. Team members discuss any helpful information they have gathered and tell how they plan to use it.

Process Qualification Level. The final agenda item is an interactive one to determine the process's qualification level. The team states the level it believes it has achieved, justifying its rating by going through that level's checklist item by item and describing the status of each. Reviewers who concur with the team's proposed rating say so. Those who do not state their reasons and give the rating they think is more appropriate. A question-and-answer session often is conducted next. The reviewers need to gain consensus on process qualification levels.

CLOSURE

At the end of the team's presentation, each reviewer can take a turn offering feedback to the team. Feedback should be specific and descriptive. Structured feedback works best. Each reviewer can comment on the one thing he or she liked best and make one request of the team (e.g., to gather more

Celebrate what you want to see more of.

—Tom Peters

data or to reexamine a certain issue). The reviewers should express suggestions in a positive way and avoid negative criticism. The reviewers' questions and comments are key to creating an atmosphere of encouragement and learning. If the team is on the wrong track, the reviewers can discuss this privately with the process owner. It is important to minimize the risk of demoralizing the team members.

When a team reaches one of the main qualification levels (5.0, 4.0), management should mark the occasion in a special way. One quality council awards a certificate, posts it in a place where everyone can see it, and describes the team's achievements in the company newsletter. Another quality council distributes pens with the name of the team and the qualification level achieved. Often, management sponsors a celebration lunch or breakfast. A celebration rewards the team members for their hard work and encourages their future efforts.

THE BENEFITS OF REGULAR REVIEWS

The job of improving processes is never over; continuous improvement is a journey, not a destination. A process-improvement review is like a port of call—a regular stopover along the way. The benefits include a renewal of everyone's commitment, a clear sense of direction, and an opportunity for productive interaction between management and the team.

*S*uccess is a journey, not a destination.

—Ben Sweetland

RENEWED COMMITMENT

Reviews renew everyone's commitment and enthusiasm. The team gets a boost from the recognition of its

In 1990, 36 percent of employees who reported to the Gallup Organization that their companies had quality programs said they did not participate in those activities. Major reasons given included a lack of available programs, not enough time to participate, irrelevant programs, and not being invited to participate.[2]

work, and management is keener on the improvement effort after seeing results. Process improvement is a quiet endeavor, and there are usually many people in an organization who do not know about it. After a process review, managers tend to mention the results achieved to others.

For the team members, working together on the presentation enlarges their perspectives and boosts morale. It involves everyone and encourages members to think about what they are doing as a team. In the course of deciding what to present to management and how to rate themselves, team members pull together in a common effort.

The review is energizing for management, too. Understanding what the team has done and the barriers it has overcome solidifies executive commitment to process improvement. Because the executive team reviews all the organization's process-improvement efforts, it gains an awareness of the combined impact of the concurrent efforts. It sees concrete evidence that process improvement is saving the organization money and improving the quality of what its customers receive.

A CLEAR SENSE OF DIRECTION

A review is not only an opportunity to look back but also an opportunity to look ahead. Setting future objectives refocuses the team and provides a clear sense of direction.

The review gives management a chance to offer guidance and information to the team. If the team is heading in the wrong direction, management can correct the course.

INTERACTION BETWEEN SENIOR MANAGEMENT AND THE TEAM

A review can open up new lines of communication between the team and management and can confirm the value of employee empowerment. The team members have a chance to talk about what they are doing in a professional way. Managers have an opportunity to ask questions and to provide clarity and support. The result usually is that the team feels appreciated and empowered, and management gains a better understanding of the nuts and bolts of the organization's processes.

TIPS

♦ Short-term checks between six-month reviews are often necessary to keep management aware of changes and difficulties. A team may not be meeting regularly; there may be difficulty determining the scope of activities, and so on. The earlier that management knows about such things, the better.

♦ Sometimes people want to combine process-improvement reviews and operations reviews, spending the first half of the session on one and the second half on the other. This arrangement does not work well, because the two kinds of reviews have different purposes, and it is difficult to shift gears that fast. An operations review is concerned with how a team has met operating targets. A process-improvement review takes a look at what the team has done to bring the process under control and meet customer expectations. It is best not to combine (or confuse) the two.

We know exactly where we want to go because
our customers will show us the way.

Jerre Stead, CEO, AT&T Global Information Solutions

Do you ever listen to your recorded voice and think, "Is that how I really sound?" Do you look at yourself in photographs or videos and feel surprised when the image does not match what you see in the bathroom mirror? Looking at yourself backward through a telescope—to discover how you really look to others—can be a difficult thing to do.

The view we have of our organizations can be equally distorted. We think that we're doing a good job, that we're providing the quality of product or service our customers want. We are often wrong.

This brief chapter encourages you to keep the telescope handy and tells why it is necessary to look backward through it at regular intervals.

REFOCUSING THE TELESCOPE

Decay is inherent in all compounded things.
Strive on with diligence.

Buddha (Prince Siddhartha)

9

The purpose of "customer-inspired quality" is to determine how our customers define quality (which may be quite different from how we define it) and to establish quantifiable ways to improve processes so that we can meet and exceed our customers' expectations.

As you progress through the steps of a process-improvement initiative, and as you refocus the telescope from an "in-out" view of the marketplace to an "out-in" look at the organization, what you perceive about many aspects of your organization changes.

MANAGEMENT PERSEVERANCE IS CRITICAL

The most important factor in the success of a process-improvement effort is perseverance by management—believing in the quest for excellence, leading the way, and supporting the efforts. Bottom-up or outside-in efforts to improve quality don't work. Only top management has the perspective and authority to issue a call to action throughout the organization and to make continuous process improvement a reality.

EMPLOYEE PARTICIPATION IS ESSENTIAL

The people who do the work are the best qualified to identify and implement improvements to it. Process improvement helps employees gain a clearer understanding of their work and how it interacts with and impacts others. Feedback systems bring employees into direct, regular contact with suppliers and customers, further enlarging their perspectives. Employees also gain access to information through process improvement, and they learn how to use data to perform analysis and make decisions.

Active, enthusiastic participation by employees is essential to the success of a process-improvement initiative. Workers know what goes wrong and where the glitches are in their processes. If they are given the training and the support, they are the best situated to develop creative and effective ideas for making positive changes.

When empowered employees become convinced that their duty is to their process, not to their boss, wonderful things begin to happen. Teams shoulder responsibility for their processes, and a new, more cooperative style of work evolves.

PROCESS-IMPROVEMENT EFFORTS CHANGE ROLES

Process-improvement efforts change the roles of managers. Processes are managed, not people. Process-improvement initiatives transform managers into process owners. Their duties shift from directing and controlling people to improving and managing processes. Working across departmental boundaries, process owners gain a new perspective of the organization as a system of interdependent processes.

PROCESS IMPROVEMENT HAS FAR-REACHING EFFECTS

The very structure of an organization is likely to change when the old organizational chart is replaced by the new view of the organization as a system of interrelated, interdependent processes. Hierarchy flattens as cross-functional improvement teams set goals for their processes and self-directed work teams perform the tasks of the organization. Fewer layers of management are needed. This happened at Federal Express, which now has only five levels of management for 90,000 employees.

Q*uality is not a thing, it's a way.*

—Elton Hubbard

Process improvement reconstructs the organization around the activities that provide products or services to customers, rather than around traditional departments or functions. As processes are streamlined, the organization is able to be more flexible and more responsive.

Looking at your organization from your customers' point of view and improving processes to enable you to meet and exceed your customers' expectations is the only way to achieve quality, because quality is defined by the customer. In the end, the customer's viewpoint is the only one that counts.

ACTION STEP

Assume that you have successfully implemented process improvement so that all outputs that customers receive consistently meet all their expectations. What effect would this have on your business?

Notes

INTRODUCTION

CHAPTER 1: GETTING OFF THE CLIFF EDGE

1. W.E. Deming, *Out of the Crisis* (Cambridge, MA: Massachusetts Institute of Technology, Center for Advanced Engineering Study, 1986), p. 3.

CHAPTER 4: PINNING DOWN THE PROTOZOA

1. Quoted in P. Dickson, *The Official Rules* (New York, Dell Publishing, 1978), p. 142.

2. O. Port, J. Carey, K. Kelly, & S.A. Forest, "Quality: Small and Midsize Companies Seize the Challenge—Not a Moment Too Soon," *Business Week,* November 30, 1992, pp. 66-72.

3. *Industry Week* (Cleveland, OH), cited in Communication Briefings, September 1995, p. 2.

4. S. Thomas, "What Is Motorola's Six Sigma Product Quality?," *Proceedings,* AAPICS International Conference, New Orleans, LA, October 8-12, 1990, pp. 27-31.

CHAPTER 6: IMPROVING THE COMMON TASKS

1. D. Greising, "Making Quality Pay," *Business Week,* August 8, 1994, p. 57.

2. M. Hammer, "The Promise of Reengineering," *Fortune,* May 3, 1993, p. 96.

3. J. Farrell, "A Practical Guide for Implementing Reengineering," *Planning Review,* March/April 1994, pp. 40-45.

CHAPTER 8: PLUGGING IN

1. J.A. Edosomwan, "Six Commandments To Empower Employees for Quality Improvement," *Industrial Engineering,* July 1992, pp. 14-15.

2. "Companies Fail To Maximize Human Resource Potential," *Industrial Engineering,* November 1990, pp. 10-12.

Index

THE WARREN BENNIS EXECUTIVE BRIEFING SERIES

*"To survive in the 21st century, we're going to need
a new generation of leaders, not managers.
This series is an exciting collection of business books
written to help your leaders meet the challenges of the new millennium."*

Dr. Warren Bennis
USC Professor and Founding Chairman, The Leadership Institute
Author, *On Becoming a Leader* and *An Invented Life*

Tailored to the needs of busy professionals and authored by subject matter experts, the *Warren Bennis Executive Briefing Series* helps leaders acquire significant knowledge in the face of information overload. All *Series* titles utilize the SuperReading comprehension/retention editing and design techniques made famous by Howard Berg, *The Guinness Book of World Records'* "World's Fastest Reader." Read these 128-page books in just two hours!

TITLES INCLUDE:

Fabled Service: Ordinary Acts, Extraordinary Outcomes	Betsy Sanders
The 21st Century Organization: Reinventing Through Reengineering	Warren Bennis/ Michael Mische
Managing Globalization in the Age of Interdependence	George Lodge
Coach to Coach: Business Lessons from the Locker Room	John Robinson
The Faster Learning Organization: Gain and Sustain the Competitive Edge	Bob Guns
The Absolutes of Leadership	Philip Crosby
Customer-Inspired Quality: Looking Backward Through the Telescope	James Shaw
InfoRelief: Stay Afloat in the InfoFlood	Maureen Malanchuk

Contact your local bookstore for all *Warren Bennis Executive Briefing Series* titles, or order directly from Pfeiffer & Company Customer Service, **1-800-274-4434**.

About the Author

James G. Shaw is founder of Shaw Resources, an executive consulting firm based in Cupertino, California. A nationally recognized consultant, he has pioneered the efforts to bring process improvement from the manufacturing floor to service industries and administrative and service functions. During the past eight years, he has guided executives of a wide variety of organizations in their efforts to achieve quality and create a customer-driven perspective.

Jim Shaw began his career as a quality engineer. He has twenty years of corporate experience in high-technology manufacturing and has held several high-level executive positions in a Fortune 500 high-technology company. He was a member of the 1994, 1995, and 1996 Boards of Examiners for the Malcolm Baldrige National Quality Award and serves on its Health Care and Education Pilot Evaluation Team. Shaw also is a member of the American Society for Quality Control, the American Marketing Association, and the Association for Quality and Participation.

He has a B.A. in Physics from the University of California, Riverside, and an M.B.A. in Finance and Quality Improvement from the University of California, Berkeley. He has written articles on quality improvement for several journals, including *Quality Progress, TQM Magazine, Strategies for Healthcare Excellence, MGM Journal,* and *Group Practice Journal.*